In the Beginning

ARCHIPELAGO

THE ORIGIN AND DISCOVERY
OF THE HAWAIIAN ISLANDS

DR. RICHARD W. GRIGG

ISLAND HERITAGE™
PUBLISHING
A DIVISION OF THE MADDEN CORPORATION

CONTENTS

THE HAWAIIAN ARCHIPELAGO
PACIFIC ISLAND PARADISE

Hawai'i is more than an island or even a cluster of islands or even a string of islands. Hawai'i is an archipelago of islands, atolls, and undersea volcanoes that stretch halfway across the western Pacific Ocean. The archipelago, officially known as the Hawaiian-Emperor Chain, is a vast armada of volcanic peaks made up of the highest mountains on Earth, which drop from snow-packed peaks to great abyssal depths; high islands that are magically beautiful, deeply eroded, and verdant with uniquely evolved ecosystems; the lonely and mostly uninhabited Northwestern Islands, the most isolated islets and atolls on Earth; and dozens of volcanic edifices that never made it to sea level or

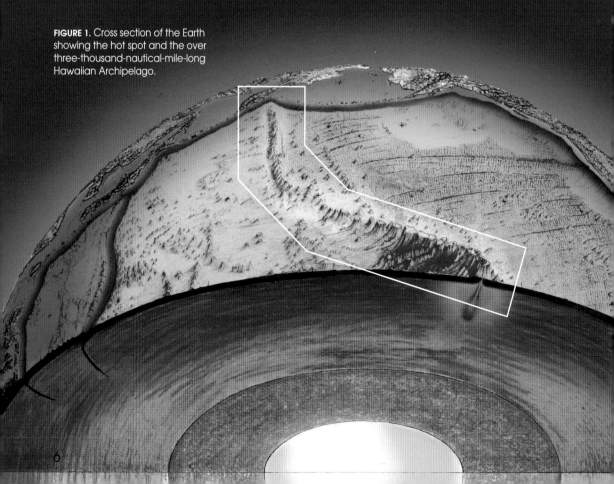

FIGURE 1. Cross section of the Earth showing the hot spot and the over three-thousand-nautical-mile-long Hawaiian Archipelago.

FIGURE 2. The Hawaiian-Emperor Chain is the longest archipelago in the world, but only 2.5 percent of the volcanoes are above sea level.

that are now drowned among the chain of Emperor Seamounts that reaches all the way to Kamchatka, where they ultimately will be swallowed up into the Aleutian Trench.

This vast chain of islands, atolls, and volcanoes is the greatest archipelago in the world (see figures 1 and 2), and this book tells the story of their volcanic origins, their long lives, and their ultimate fates. For more than seventy million years, they have slowly drifted more than three thousand miles northwest across the Pacific Ocean on an oceanic plate of the Earth's crust, drifting like all the continents, to a point where they will return from whence they came, pushed and pulled down in a process called subduction into the western edge of the Pacific Ring of Fire, into a deep trench and then even deeper still, into the molten mantle below the Earth's crust. Fire to fire. Dust to dust. Life to death.

It is also a story of the colonists, first the marine plants and animals, followed by those that would inhabit the lands, and finally the great human discoverers, first the Polynesians, then the European explorers, and then all of us who live or visit here today. It is a story of many origins and of many paths traveled, from the first Hawaiian island to the many stories that brought each one of us to where we are today and to what we all might agree is paradise.

CHAPTER 1

ORIGINS

IN THE BEGINNING

Long before the Greek god Prometheus dared seize the fire from Mount Olympus and carry part of heaven back to Earth, the Earth itself had created a paradise of islands located in the middle of the Pacific Ocean. Some seventy million years before the Greeks created their myths, about the time the age of the dinosaurs was coming to a close, a new world of islands was starting to brew deep within the mantle of the Earth.

The Earth is but a molten mass of iron core wrapped by a thick viscous mantle of lava, overlain by a hard but pliable crust. Within the mantle churns huge convection cells of molten mass driven by the heat generated by radioactive decay of the hot elements like uranium, radium, strontium, potassium, and carbon. Adding to the cauldron are zillions of neutrinos, high-energy particles produced by the sun and exploding stars, that zing through the Earth every second.

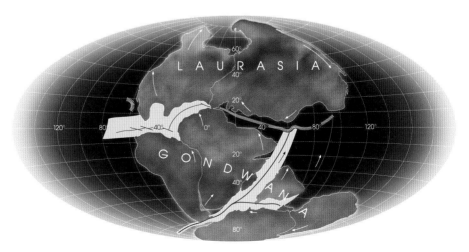

FIGURE 4. Pangaea splits to form the supercontinents of Laurasia and Gondwana and ultimately seven continents and four oceans.

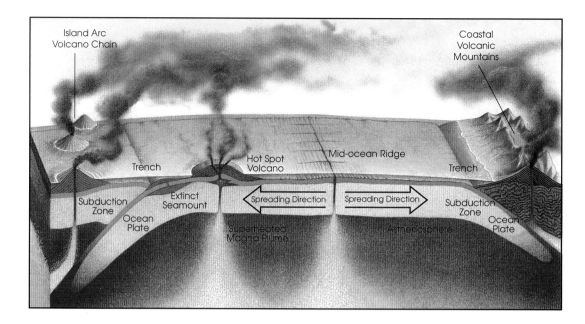

From the beginning of our restless Earth, convection cells have been revolving relentlessly within the mantle. Their churning motion is thought to be a major force in producing continental drift, the motion of the overlying continents and oceanic plates. All land masses were once connected into a supercontinent called Pangaea, but for the past three hundred million years they have been drifting apart, having today produced seven separate continents and four great oceans. But to understand the Pacific Ocean, we must back up to Pangaea splitting apart into two supercontinents, Gondwana and Laurasia, separated by a sliver of primordial ocean called the Tethys Sea (figure 4).

The Tethys Sea would later expand into the Pacific and eventually be encircled by a vast ring of fire defined by volcanic mountain ranges and deep trenches (figure 5). A midoceanic ridge zone would push out huge slabs of crust, or plates, that would grow and grow into an ever-widening oceanic crust that eventually became an enormous basin—the Pacific Ocean. The trenches served to constrain the expanding crusts by swallowing up their edges as they pushed against the surrounding continents. Somewhere in the middle of this massive new ocean, about seventy million years ago, one of the Earth's convection cells pushed up a powerful plume of lava that ruptured the sea bottom, breaking through the crust and producing the first Hawaiian island.

Our story of the Hawaiian Archipelago begins in the middle of the Pacific, the biggest ocean of all. Like the rest of the Earth, the archipelago had no name, until millions of years later, a proud but wandering clan of seafaring explorers followed Pacific stars in their sailing canoes across the ocean where they discovered a new land. They had found a piece of the heaven on Earth created by Prometheus. It was to become Hawai'i, and they were to become the Hawai-

FIGURE 5. Expansion of the Pacific Ocean and the formation of the first Hawaiian Island, both driven by mantle convection and a hot spot.

ians. But to fully appreciate the majesty of these most beautiful islands in the world, we must first explore their origins as well and look carefully at their long and fascinating history.

ISLANDS BORN BY UNDERSEA FIRE

The Hawaiian hot spot is one of about twenty-five or more major hot spots that dot the surface of the Earth. They mark the heads of convection cells in the mantle. They are hot points of upwelling plumes of mantle forming a thunderhead pattern of upward flow. As though the Earth is venting its internal heat, the hot plumes push up against the undersurface of the crust beneath the ocean, forming broad rises, or swells, on the ocean bottom. Like a subterranean blowtorch, the plumes thin the crust and then fracture it into vents, which ultimately rupture through the bottom, producing undersea volcanoes (figure 6).

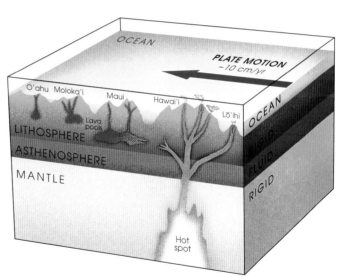

FIGURE 6.
Island formation over the Hawaiian hot spot. The hot spot is believed to be fixed within the Earth's mantle. Slow drift of overlying crust (lithosphere) to the northwest carries volcanoes off the hot spot and forms a long trail of islands.

The most easterly vent is now forming an undersea volcano about twenty miles east of the Big Island of Hawai'i called Lō'ihi. Although Lō'ihi is already thirteen thousand feet above the seafloor, it will not break the ocean's surface for another fifty thousand or more years. Its volcanic summit is three thousand feet deep. Lō'ihi is but the last in a very long string of volcanoes. However, before exploring Lō'ihi further, we should first look back in time to the beginning of the entire chain of islands, the Hawaiian Archipelago.

The Hawaiian Archipelago is the longest, oldest, and best-studied chain of islands in the world. It is also the most isolated group of islands in the world, and as will be discussed in chapters 5 and 6, this is a fact of extreme importance in understanding its life forms (flora and fauna) and of course, human occupation during the last twelve hundred years or so.

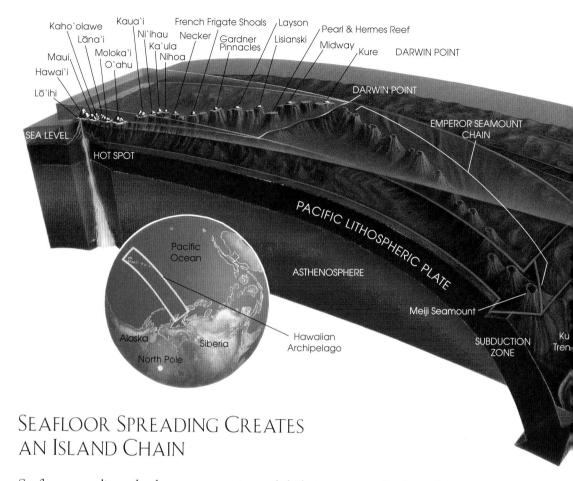

SEAFLOOR SPREADING CREATES AN ISLAND CHAIN

Seafloor spreading, also known as continental drift, is not completely understood, but as mentioned above, it is likely caused by a combination of factors including the frictional drag produced by convection cells on the undersurface of the crust and the push and pull of oceanic plates. The push comes from new crustal plates forming along spreading centers that produce elongate rifts that encircle the oceans. The plates also produce the pull but only after millions of years drifting across ocean basins where they finally subduct, drawn down into deep trenches (figure 7).

In the case of the Hawaiian Archipelago, what we have then is a relatively fixed hot spot underlying a slowly moving plate of oceanic crust. The hot spot is believed to originate about fifteen hundred miles within the mantle, whereas the floor of the Pacific is moving to the northwest over the hot spot at a relatively constant speed of three to four inches (eight to ten centimeters) a year and has been doing so for more than seventy million years. Over this time, the hot spot has been issuing forth a new Hawaiian Island or undersea volcano about once every million years, producing all told about 107 volcanic edifices, all moving from southeast to northwest as silent passengers on a great undersea conveyor belt.

FIGURE 7. A hot spot and subduction trench mark the beginning and the end of the Hawaiian Archipelago.

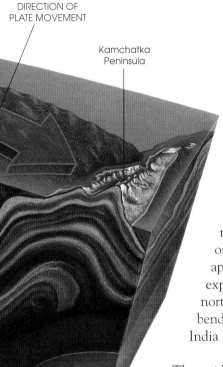

DIRECTION OF
PLATE MOVEMENT

Kamchatka
Peninsula

ASTHENOSPHERE

The first known Hawaiian Island to emerge from the Hawaiian hot spot was Meiji volcano (today a drowned coral island or guyot; see chapter 4) approximately seventy million–plus years ago. Movement of the Pacific Plate has transported Meiji from its original location where the Big Island of Hawaiʻi sits today to the edge of Kamchatka, more than three thousand nautical miles northwest, where it is in the process of being subducted below the North American Plate at the far eastern edge of Russia.

The trajectory of the Hawaiian hot spot trail of volcanoes follows an almost straight geographic pathway. The one exception to this linear trend is a bend that occurs at approximately the fifty-million-year mark, which might be explained by a shift in the direction of plate propagation from north to northwest (figures 2 and 7). The exact cause of the bend is conjectural but may have been due to the collision of India (once an island in the Indian Ocean) with Asia.

The evidence that connects all 107 Hawaiian volcanoes is somewhat technical, but I mention it here briefly because it is so compelling. First, there is age progression. Each island moving to the northwest in the Hawaiian Chain is older than the one behind it. Further up the chain past the bend lie the Emperor Seamounts, and they too are progressively older moving to the north. Then there is something called paleomagnetism that is a measure of the latitude at the time the molten lavas of each volcano congealed. The Earth's magnetic field at this point of their origin was sealed within hardening rock. The paleolatitude of the origin of many of the Hawaiian volcanoes "backdates" to about 20 degrees north latitude, which is also the latitude of the hot spot. Finally, the chemical signatures of the lavas of the Hawaiian Islands and undersea volcanoes are extremely similar, suggesting a common origin.

The next three chapters will discuss the individual islands and how they have changed over their long history. But first, let us turn to Lōʻihi volcano, where we can begin with the present and then travel progressively up the volcanic chain. By so doing, we will actually be moving backward through time in terms of the age of the islands or seamounts, until we finally reach the end at Meiji Guyot, which as we now know, was really the beginning. Prometheus himself would be amazed to learn just what kind of a heaven he created on Earth.

CHAPTER 2

LŌʻIHI
THE NEXT HAWAIIAN ISLAND

DIVE TO LŌʻIHI

Lōʻihi volcano lies deep beneath the Pacific Ocean, slumbering some three thousand feet below the surface, just twenty miles offshore due east of the south coast of the Big Island of Hawaiʻi (figure 9). We now know that Lōʻihi is volcanically active. It is a site of frequent earthquakes, volcanic eruptions, and large landslides. It is almost certainly an embryonic island. Lōʻihi, which means "long" in Hawaiian, is growing foot by foot by the accumulation of eruptive lavas, but it is also wasting away due to downslides of volcanic debris. For every foot that Lōʻihi gains, more than 90 percent of the lava is lost due to down-slope erosion. Its birth as a Hawaiian Island almost seems painful, as if it is laboring to reach the surface under the weight of three thousand feet of water, which is one hundred times the weight of the Earth's atmosphere. Presently, Lōʻihi is sixteen miles long and eight miles wide. Its elevation above the Hawaiian sea bottom is 12,320 feet. On a relative scale, Lōʻihi is already a very large undersea mountain, and yet it will take another fifty thousand or so years to reach the surface. A mere blink in geological time.

Lōʻihi volcano was first discovered in 1955 by Kenneth Emory during a routine oceanographic survey of Hawaiʻi's undersea geology. At the time, it wasn't known to be volcanically active. But then, during the mid 1970s, a number of earthquake swarms were recorded on the Big Island and were identified as originating from an epicenter that coincided with the summit of Lōʻihi. It would take almost ten more years before an ocean expedition could be organized and funded that included, for the first time, a deep-submergence vehicle, in this case, the *Alvin*. The *Alvin* submersible is capable of carrying three people to depths up to ten thousand feet. As luck would have it, I was one of seven divers on that first team of scientists who would make the maiden dives to Lōʻihi in February 1987 (figure 8).

FIGURE 8. Launch of the *Alvin* Submersible, February 15, 1987.

FIGURE 9. Map of the major high Hawaiian Islands showing the location of Lōʻihi submarine volcano, twenty miles east of the Big Island of Hawaiʻi.

Our ocean quest was to find the answers to a number of intriguing and important questions. Could we verify that Lōʻihi will be Hawaiʻi's next island? Is the volcanic activity at Lōʻihi evidence that the hot spot is on the move or splitting up? Or is the eastward jump in eruptive activity simply more evidence that the crust on which it lies is slowing inching northwestward over the Hawaiian hot spot (figure 6)? Would we find oases of deep-ocean life on Lōʻihi, or would it be barren? Would Lōʻihi be too new to support lush communities of mussels and clams, huge sea worms, numerous fishes, and other exotic sea life well known from other undersea hot volcanic centers or rift zones? What would Lōʻihi, the only known site of an embryonic island in Hawaiʻi, tell us about the birth of all the other Hawaiian Islands that must have gone through the same phase of development, millions of years earlier? What answers would we find to questions that we had not even thought to ask?

My first deep dive to the summit of Lō'ihi was on the morning of February 15, 1987, in the *Alvin*. My sub-mates were Professor Alex Malahoff and the pilot scientist Ken Swanson. The first twenty-five minutes were very quiet as we sank until the last glimmer of sunlight was lost, deeper and deeper into a black and gloomy place. At a depth of thirty-two hundred feet, our instruments showed that we were approaching the bottom. A water temperature gauge inside the sub started to jump upward: 35 degrees Celsius, then 40, then 50. Then, faintly illuminated in the glow of *Alvin's* reflected light, a miniature volcanic cone began to slowly come into focus. We seemed to be enveloped in a warm plume of water streaming upward. *Alvin's* light beams were shimmering through the water. We had landed in a field of hydrothermal vents all spewing fountains of hot water into an otherwise frigid and lightless sea. The field of vents looked like miniature chimneys or strange, upside-down-ice-cream-cone-shaped anthills (figure 10). We were to learn from later dives that they are actually minivents leaking hot-water fluids, effusing upward and slowly building cones of metal rich compounds. Several years later, these vents would be named "Pele's vents" by pilots of Hawai'i Undersea Research Laboratory (HURL) in honor of the Hawaiian goddess of the volcano, Madam Pele.

FIGURE 10. Pele's vents on the summit of Lō'ihi volcano at a depth of thirty-two hundred feet.

The scene outside our submersible ports looked primordial, eerie, almost ominous. There was no life. Nothing moved except the shimmering water. Blobs of tiny yellow particles drifted up and floated above us in the vent water, spreading out over the flanks of the volcano and then ever so slowly settling back to the bottom, covering the floor with a Jovian blanket of yellow and magenta snow. It seemed as though our submersible had somehow been transported to another planet.

We backed the vessel off the vent field and settled to the bottom in an area below it. The bottom here was covered with a thicker organic mat. It was like spongy carpet. At once we maneuvered the robotic arm of the submersible and scooped up a sample of the porous substance. Later work would show that the mat and colorful blanket of "snow" consisted entirely of primitive marine bacteria. Our mission that day would include collecting many bottom and water samples, taking cores in the bottom, measuring temperature, and, of course, taking many photographs and recording observations.

MASS WASTING

From this point near the summit field at a depth of 3,250 feet, Alex, Ken, and I descended slowly along the north ridge of the volcano. Our six-hour trek covered almost three miles of terrain down to almost 6,000 feet. The most striking thing about our survey was the degree to which the bottom was covered by pure rubble. Apparently, eruptions at the summit are instantly cooled, causing the lava to crack open forming boulders and irregular rubble (talus). Massive sheets of talus spread out in all directions from the ridgeline. The landscape looked like the aftermath of a huge landslide or, more likely, many, many landslides (figure 11). Alex called it mass wasting. Lō'ihi appeared to be losing ground almost as fast as it was being produced.

FIGURE 11. Eruptions of lava on the summit of Lō'ihi produce blankets of landsliding volcanic debris. Up to 90 percent of Lō'ihi's flanks are covered by massive sheets of this kind of broken and slippery talus.

Between five thousand and six thousand feet, we started seeing more intact pillow lava flows. They looked like overlapping pancakes: smooth, round, layer upon layer, densely packed, and stable. It appeared as though we had reached the beginning of a solid and stable foundation, the very stability on which the future of the young volcano would depend.

The geological significance of what we had observed was the degree to which the emerging undersea volcano was undergoing mass wasting. The fields of talus looked like ball bearings, almost slippery, over which new lava flows or landslides would cascade. Later research would reveal that much of the architecture of all the Hawaiian Islands is a result of frequent and sometimes massive landslides, and, as we will see in later chapters, the landslides are not always limited to those that originate undersea.

LIFE ON LŌʻIHI

Our maiden dive to Lōʻihi also produced some astonishing biological findings. The summit of Lōʻihi volcano is extremely toxic. Not only is the summit water heated to as much as 90 degrees Celsius, but it is also devoid of oxygen. The bacterial mats consist of mostly dead bacterial filaments. Dr. David Karl has described them as a "fossilized" bacterial community. Only 1 to 2 percent of the tubular filaments contained recognizable organic matter. The bacterial cells might be short-lived or episodic in nature, possibly living only during quiescent periods of the volcano. Analysis of the vent fluids we collected during our dives showed it to be extremely acidic, containing 140 times more carbon dioxide than normal seawater. Methane, iron, and sulfur compounds were also found to be abnormally high. The summit of Lōʻihi may be the most naturally polluted place in Hawaiʻi.

Fortunately, the poisonous zone around the summit of Lōʻihi does not extend to greater depths, especially in stable areas where outcrops of solid lava are covered with large gold and pink corals. These stable patches are like biological oases surrounded by broken debris fields, the remnants of frequent summit or ridgeline landslides. Similar patches of life exist on land, between and among the lava flows of the active volcanoes on the Big Island; they are known as *kīpuka*.

Also fascinating is the apparent relation between the heated summit vent water and the highly porous debris fields. Heat within the core of the volcano appears to act like a huge built-in pump. Water surrounding the flanks of the volcano can percolate into the porous shield. Once inside, it would gradually be heated, causing it to slowly rise and concentrate toward the summit. Once there, it would naturally escape through a diffuse system of vents.

On one of the later dives during the February 1987 expedition, Dr. David Karl and the pilot came face-to-face with an extraordinary fish. What looked like a giant white toad was actually *Sladenia remiger*, a rare species of monk fish. Perched on fins that acted as feet, it sat motionless, almost transfixed on the bottom, peering back at the submarine with huge blue eyes. It seemed like the proverbial deer in the headlights, only this time blinded by the searchlights of the *Alvin*. Dave was able to reach out with the robotic claw and grab one of its "feet" before it could swim away. It would turn out to be only the third specimen of this species ever collected in the world (figure 12).

Another tantalizing discovery, made by Dr. Mike Garcia on one of the later dives, was the presence of alkalic lavas from the summit of Lō'ihi. Alkalic lavas contain more dissolved gases than the more normal lavas (theoleiitic basalts) that are known to build more than 95 percent of all Hawaiian volcanoes. This finding might explain the extremely high concentration of carbon dioxide gas found in the vent waters rising from Pele's vents. Some of the rocks we brought to the surface on our dive actually fizzed when they were broken open. The surface, of course, doesn't have the pressure of three thousand feet of water, and hence the gas locked inside the rocks (in a liquid state) was suddenly able to escape like bubbles of soda gas in a soft drink when the top has been popped. Alkalic eruptions closer to the surface could be potentially explosive.

Another intriguing fact about the alkalic lavas is that they are normally only found in the dying days of a Hawaiian volcano. Could this mean that Lō'ihi could soon die, stillborn within the sea before it breaks the surface? If so, where and when will the hot spot next break through the bottom crust to produce yet another volcano, itself becoming a new island? Or could the alkalic lavas on Lō'ihi mark the death of the hot spot itself? If so, the Big Island would be the last Hawaiian Island to form in the archipelago. Given that 106 volcanoes have preceded it over the last seventy million years, the prospect of Lō'ihi dying before it is born seems hardly probable. I am betting that Lō'ihi will someday make it to the surface.

A final reflection on our voyage to Lō'ihi goes back to the primordial and exotic conditions for life that exist on the summit. There is no oxygen in the chemically rich water, and it is heated up to 90 degrees Celsius. It almost sounds like the "warm little pond" that Charles Darwin imagined when he theorized about where and how life first evolved on the planet. Indeed, the only evidence of life that we found on the summit was mats of extremely primitive bacteria, some belonging to the primordial family known as Archaea. Almost more amazing is the great contrast that the environment on Lō'ihi's summit makes with the lush and verdant communities of plants and animals that live on all the rest of the Hawaiian volcanoes, both under the sea and on the land. This paradise of life is the subject of chapters 5 and 6.

FIGURE 12. Dr. Alex Malahoff holding *Sladenia remiger* on board the University of Hawai'i mother ship. Note the antennae on the snout of the monk fish. At its tip is a tiny light that lures in prey for this ambush predator.

CHAPTER 3

THE MAJOR HIGH HAWAIIAN ISLANDS
HAWAIʻI TO NIʻIHAU

THEORIES OF ISLAND FORMATION

While plate movement over a relatively fixed hot spot is universally accepted today as the theory that best explains the origin of the Hawaiian Archipelago, it is interesting both culturally and historically to explore other ideas of island origin that existed before plate tectonics was discovered in the 1960s and '70s.

In 1849, James Dana, who was the first geologist to visit the Hawaiian Islands, observed a gradient in the degree of erosion along the island chain. Dana believed that all the major high Hawaiian volcanoes erupted simultaneously, and he attributed the differences between them to erosion and their order of extinction, which he imagined was age-progressive down the chain from Kauaʻi to the Big Island of Hawaiʻi. This view would explain why the island of Kauaʻi appears to be the most eroded island, which it is (figure 13), as well as the fact that the down-chain islands of Oʻahu, Molokaʻi, Maui, and the Big Island look progressively younger. Interestingly, this view was consistent with early Hawaiian legends that placed the home of the goddess Pele first on Kauaʻi and then progressively eastward, island by island, to the Big Island, where she resides today. Both ideas explain the morphology of the major high Hawaiian Islands but both misrepresent their true ages.

A third interpretation is that of a propagating fracture that moved down the chain to the southeast from Kauaʻi to the Big Island to create the major high islands. This idea would also describe their morphology, and it would be age-progressive, yielding younger islands to the southeast, which is true, but for one serious problem: no such fracture is known to exist. This theory, and Dana's, of course, were based on the assumptions that the Earth was static and that the Earth's crust was stationary.

FIGURE 13. Kauaʻi's Nā Pali coast has been deeply eroded by over five million years of rain, wind, and waves.

Then in 1960, Harry Hess and Robert Dietz revolutionized Earth science with their famous theory of seafloor spreading. The Earth's crust was shown to consist of several dozen mobile plates capable of rifting islands, and even continents, great distances over the surface of the Earth (see chapter 1). Building on this theory, John Tuzo Wilson proposed that the Hawaiian Islands were formed by the Earth's crust moving northwest over a relatively fixed point of upwelling lava. Wilson theorized that this source of heat melted the Pacific Plate and produced a linear chain of seamounts and islands. The term hot spot was later coined by Eric Christofferson in 1968, and he extended Wilson's theory to include the Emperor Seamounts. Finally, in 1972, W. Jason Morgan proposed that hot spots are produced by thermal plumes originating deep within the Earth's mantle. Morgan identified about twenty hot spots on the Earth and suggested they are fixed relative to one another.

DEEP TIME

The birth of each Hawaiian island is only the beginning of a long history marked by very long periods of gradual but continual change, punctuated sometimes by catastrophic events that may take only seconds to occur. Both are equally important sculptors in shaping the unique architecture and fate of any given island. Catastrophic events like tsunamis, earthquakes, or landslides are easy to imagine since they commonly occur (on a global scale) within human lifetimes. Gradual change both geologically and biologically (evolution) is so incredibly slow that it challenges human understanding and even belief. Take for example the time it must have taken for the Colorado River to carve out the Grand Canyon in Arizona. And in Hawai'i, how long will it take Lō'ihi to break the ocean surface and become an island and then drift off the hot spot to the end of the island chain and then keep drifting to final subduction beneath Kamchatka? The answers are about fifty thousand years, then thirty million years, and finally about seventy million years. How can human minds imagine such immensities?

And in biology, consider the complexity and grandeur of the human eye. How could anything so perfect and complex simply evolve? Many would argue that it must have been created by the hand of God. Yet consider the eye of a giant squid. It works essentially the same way as the human eye. Or consider the pigment cells in algae or corals that are light-adapted or have light-specialized behavior. How many trillions of trials and errors of biological mutation were required to produce such sensitivity? And how long did those trillion changes of molecular DNA take to transpire?

Time is the great mystifier that defies and often denies our ability to understand such miracles. Yet by projecting one's mind into the murky past or unknown future of both geological and biological evolution, it is possible to imagine such things. In a way, by mentally going there, we extend our own mortality to a virtual immortality. To truly understand the origin and history of the Hawaiian Archipelago, we might begin by reconstructing the youngest island of Hawai'i, first by emergence, then submergence, and then factoring in the effects of uplift and erosion. And we must continuously think about the huge amount of time that it took.

EMERGENCE, SUBSIDENCE, UPLIFT, AND EROSION

The Big Island of Hawai'i is the end result of six volcanoes, each separated in age and location, but all gradually building and coalescing over a period of six hundred thousand years to become one magnificent volcanic edifice (figure 14).

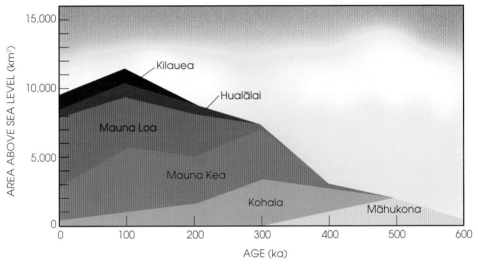

FIGURE 14. Plot of age (in thousands of years) versus the area occupied by the six volcanoes that have built the Big Island of Hawai'i.

The Māhukona volcano began forming about six hundred thousand years ago but only erupted for about three hundred thousand years before it was overgrown by the Kohala volcano, then Mauna Kea, Mauna Loa, Hualālai, and Kīlauea in that order. Today, Māhukona volcano is actually underwater, leaving only five volcanoes above sea level. Of these, Kohala is the oldest, and as we will see, the most eroded. Mauna Kea and Mauna Loa are the two biggest, and Hualālai and Kīlauea are the two youngest. All were built by the gradual accumulation of thin flows of *pāhoehoe* (smooth, unbroken lava) and *'a'ā* (stony and rough lava), eruption upon eruption, layer upon layer, millennium upon millennium. The Big Island is the largest island in the chain. In fact, it is the largest island ever produced within the chain, and it is still growing. From top to bottom, it is thirty-two thousand feet high, higher than Mount Everest.

All the islands have been built by the same stationary hot spot. The hot spot is actually the top of a deep mantle plume (see figure 1 in the preface), but as it nears the surface of the Earth, it begins to split up into separate fractures. Its emergence almost looks like the head of a hydra or a multiheaded fire-breathing dragon (see figure 6 in chapter 1). Counting Lō'ihi, the distance between the active volcanoes on the Big Island is on the order of twenty-five miles. As for temperature, the erupting lavas at the surface can exceed 2000 degrees Fahrenheit. The hot spot is truly hot! As the Pacific Plate moves over the hot spot, it carries with it each new island.

The mantle plume or hot spot has not only created a long chain of islands but it has also heated, thinned, and uplifted the crust to produce a broad swell three hundred to four hundred miles wide, which itself rises about four thousand to five thousand feet above the bottom of the surrounding Pacific Ocean. The individual islands are all superimposed on the swell and centered approximately along its midline. The largest volcanoes on the Big Island, Mauna Kea and Mauna Loa, have each added about ten thousand feet of elevation on top of the swell. The length of the swell has been traced to the end of the island chain, though it gradually deepens along the way.

At this point, it is necessary to introduce the idea of isostacy. In geology, isostacy is the balance between upward and downward forces on land or sea. For example, volcanic eruptions make an island get bigger and taller, but they also push it down due to the added weight of the lava. A simpler example would be the lowering of a boat in water as more people get on board. In the case of the Hawaiian Islands, since they are built by volcanic loading, the underlying crust is depressed downward. As the islands get bigger due to added layers of lava, they also subside due to isostatic adjustment. This process also serves to flex the Pacific Plate downward directly below the hot spot. As a consequence, as the islands are slowly built, they are also sinking to a point of isostatic equilibrium. The highest volcano on the Big Island is Mauna Kea. Its elevation is 13,792 feet, but over the time of its creation, it has subsided at least 4,000 feet. We know this because fossil coral reefs have been discovered off its west coast at a depth of 4,000 feet, and coral reefs only grow within 150 feet of the surface!

FIGURE 15. A model of bottom contours created by isostatic subsidence of the Big Island of Hawai'i.

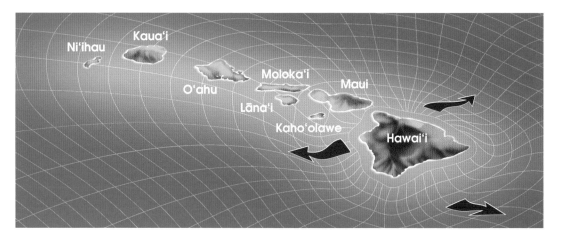

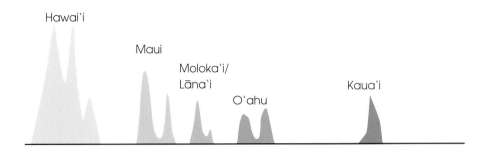

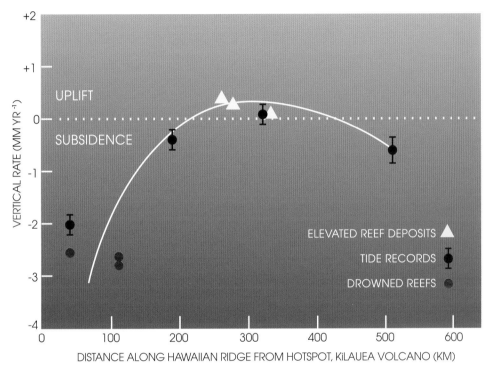

FIGURE 16. A model of subsidence and uplift (flexure) of the major Hawaiian Islands based on drowned or elevated fossil coral reefs and tide records.

Subsidence of the Big Island has also caused the underlying Pacific Plate to flex and bend. Surrounding the Big Island (again superimposed on the swell) is a deep moat and arch system that extends outward about 250 miles. The moat first descends to a depth of sixteen thousand to eighteen thousand feet but then gradually bows up about one thousand feet shallower to a surrounding arch. The moat and arch are also known as the Hawaiian Deep and the lithospheric bulge. Now if all of this wasn't complicated enough, another effect of isostatic subsidence is to uplift islands downstream from the hot spot. Elevated coral reefs on Lānaʻi, Molokaʻi, and Oʻahu provide the evidence of uplift of these three islands as they drift northwestward on the Pacific Plate over the bulge. The schematic model in figure 16 illustrates these effects on the major high Hawaiian Islands.

Compared to the amount of subsidence below the Big Island (four thousand feet), the uplift of Lāna'i and Moloka'i has only been several hundred feet. O'ahu is past the top of the bulge and is now only uplifted about ninety feet. Kaua'i appears to have cleared the bulge and is once again subsiding but at a much slower rate. Beyond Kaua'i, all the way to the end of the archipelago, the chain is slowly sinking, apparently the result of slow cooling of the underlying Pacific Plate.

Another volcanic process to consider in reconstructing the history of the high major Hawaiian Islands is something called rejuvenated volcanism, or posterosional eruption. As the islands move off the hot spot, their connection to the mantle plume is severed. Above the point of decapitation, a thin but hot and viscous pond, or lens, of lava appears to be dragged along under each island mass as it drifts to the northwest. As a consequence, a secondary and later stage of eruptive activity often takes place about two hundred miles downstream of the hot spot. About two dozen of these eruptions have taken place on both O'ahu and Kaua'i and are responsible for many small cinder cones that have become famous landmarks. On O'ahu the most well known are Diamond Head and Punchbowl Crater. Both are only several hundred thousand years old, whereas O'ahu's major volcanoes, the Ko'olau and Wai'anae ranges, are about two to four million years old. It is interesting that the distance of about two hundred miles downstream roughly corresponds with the distance to the bulge, suggesting that the bulge could have weakened or fractured the overlying island. On O'ahu, erosion of the island mass for the last four million years would have also caused it to wear down or "thin," possibly reducing the pressure on its underlying pool of lava. It is possible that O'ahu could erupt again in the future!

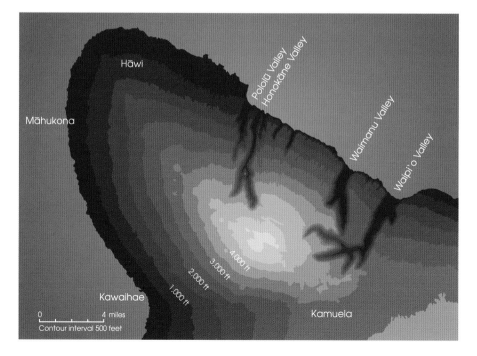

FIGURE 17. Differences in stream-cutting erosion between windward and leeward coasts are nowhere more pronounced than on Kohala volcano on the Big Island.

FIGURE 18.
The great Pali cliffs and windward coastal plain on O'ahu illustrate the pronounced differences between windward and leeward stream erosion. The wide windward plain is also a testament to the power of coastal wave cutting. The peaks in the middle of the plain are examples of rejuvenated, posterosional volcanism.

Erosion is the last process to consider in understanding the geological history of the eight major islands. Short-term instantaneous losses in island mass such as slumping or landslides can sometimes be locally catastrophic, but far more important in terms of total island deconstruction and loss of island mass to the sea is the incomprehensibly slow but highly destructive impacts of weathering from stream erosion and wave cutting at the shorelines. The multiplying effect of time and weathering over extraordinarily long periods of time takes an enormous toll. Kohala volcano on the Big Island is one of the best examples of how time and weather have altered an island landscape over the last approximately six hundred thousand years: The deep stream-cut valleys on the windward northeast face of Kohala are between one thousand and twenty-five hundred feet deep, but the shallow gulches on the westward lee slope are only one hundred feet deep. The northeastern slope has been exposed to much heavier rainfall and much stronger and more persistent wave action than the leeward coast. The northeastern shore of Kohala between Waipi'o and Pololū valleys appears to have been cut back nearly a mile by wave erosion, producing a broad offshore shelf and steep sea cliffs between the valleys (figure 17).

Another example over even longer periods of time (approximately four million years) is the difference between the windward and leeward sides of the island of O'ahu (figure 18). The highly sculptured amphitheater-shaped valleys on the windward coast versus the more gently sloping topographies on the lee side of the island clearly show the differential effects of stream erosion. The very wide coastal plain on the windward side is thought to be primarily due to wave cutting. Very early in the history of O'ahu, a large landslide in the area off Kailua and Kāne'ohe towns may have also contributed to the mass wasting that has occurred there.

Perhaps the best examples of both stream erosion and wave cutting is found off Kaua'i, the oldest of the major islands, gauged to be approximately five million years old. The spectacular Nā Pali cliffs (figure 19) are one of the steepest and most highly etched landscapes in the islands. Their steepness is a result of wave cutting, while their sculpturing is entirely due to stream erosion. Ultimately these two processes, along with subsidence, will reduce all of the high islands to low islets and finally flat coral islands, but that will take about ten million years or more. We know this because it has already happened in the Northwestern Hawaiian Islands and Emperor Seamounts, which is the subject of the next chapter.

CHANGES IN SEA LEVEL

Changes in historical sea level have also played an extremely important role in eroding, cutting, and shaping the shorelines of the major Hawaiian Islands. In the Northwestern Hawaiian Islands, the effects of wave cutting and erosion on atolls and submerged banks have been even greater, as we will see in the next chapter. To fully appreciate the impacts of sea level, it is first necessary to know that in the last two million years, during the Pleistocene ice ages, sea level has fluctuated up and down about twenty times and by as much as four hundred feet. Presently we are in a warm period, or interglacial period, and sea level is at a peak elevation, but during the glacial maximum of a typical ice age, a four-hundred-foot lowering of sea level would not be unusual. During such times, the shorelines of the islands would have existed at locations that are four hundred feet deeper than sea level today. Every feature we know on the coastlines of today, like surf sites, coves, rocky points, or bays would have been high and dry. For example, during the last ice age twenty-one thousand years ago, Kāne'ohe Bay was a dusty plain almost four hundred feet above the shoreline. Also back then, the islands of Maui, Lāna'i, Kaho'olawe, and Moloka'i would have been connected in one super island called Maui Nui (figure 20).

In contrast to how a lower sea level changed the Hawaiian Islands, we might also consider conditions that existed in the recent past when sea level was higher, as it was during the last interglacial warm period about one hundred twenty-five thousand years ago. At that time, sea level is thought to have been about twenty feet higher than it is today. Much of the evidence for this condition comes from O'ahu, where coral reefs are found all around the island on lowland plains, particularly on the leeward coast (figure 21).

Today almost all the elevated Hawaiian Islands are surrounded by drowned shelves that were cut by wave erosion during lowered stands of the sea. Some of these shelves support large beds of black coral or thick deposits of sand. Others are excellent fishing grounds for snapper and grouper or other deep-water

FIGURE 19. The Nā Pali cliffs on Kaua'i are clearly one of the most stunning and beautiful settings in the world.

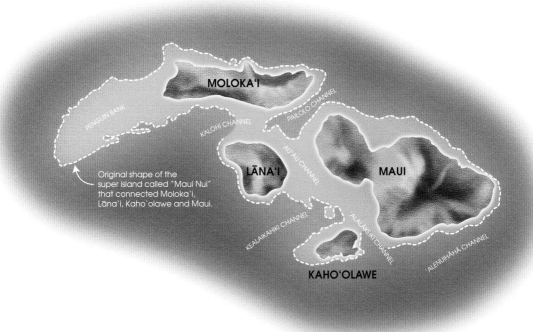

FIGURE 20. During the last ice age, twenty thousand years ago, Maui, Kaho'olawe, Lāna'i, and Moloka'i were connected by way of land bridges that were above sea level.

resources. At greater depths, below any past sea levels, are the vast undersea volcanic mountains that make up the Hawaiian Ridge and our island foundations. In fact, more than 97.5 percent of the Hawaiian volcanoes' volume is underwater! (figure 22)

Thus far our voyage to the Hawaiian Archipelago has only explored the Main Hawaiian Islands (MHI) and the forces associated with their origin and destruction. The MHI are sometimes called the major eight. They include the Big Island (Hawai'i), Maui, Kaho'olawe, Lāna'i, Moloka'i, O'ahu, Kaua'i and Ni'ihau. Now, considering only the land above sea level, the major eight islands comprise 99 percent of the area of the entire chain, however, they only represent about six million years of island history. This, of course, is less than 10 percent the age of the entire archipelago. The remaining 1 percent of the land area above sea level occurs in the Northwestern Hawaiian Islands (NWHI), aptly called the Low Islands, or sometimes the Leeward Islands. The NWHI consist of four small islets, five nearly flat coral islands, and numerous shallow banks and seamounts that are underwater.

Taken together, the MHI and the NWHI extend nearly fourteen hundred miles across the north Pacific Ocean, ranging from the Big Island at 20 degrees north latitude to Kure Atoll at almost 30 degrees north. In spite of their impressive length, these islands still only represent less than half of the entire archipelago. The rest of the chain consists of the Emperor Seamounts that begin north of Kure Atoll, where they extend another two thousand miles almost to the foot of Russia. There, below the Kamchatka Peninsula, Meiji Guyot is perched on the edge of the Aleutian-Kamchatka Trench, where it is slowly sinking (subducting) below the Asian continent. The geography of the archipelago can thus be divided into three major sections: the MHI, the NWHI, and the Emperor Seamounts. In the remaining chapters of our voyage, we revisit each leg of the chain in historic and biological detail, and examine the life in the sea and on the land, in the present as well as the past. And now, the story really gets interesting!

FIGURE 21. O'ahu Island, where elevated coral reef deposits are shown in light brown. The entire 'Ewa Plain and Pearl Harbor were at one time underwater and supported widespread and abundant coral reefs.

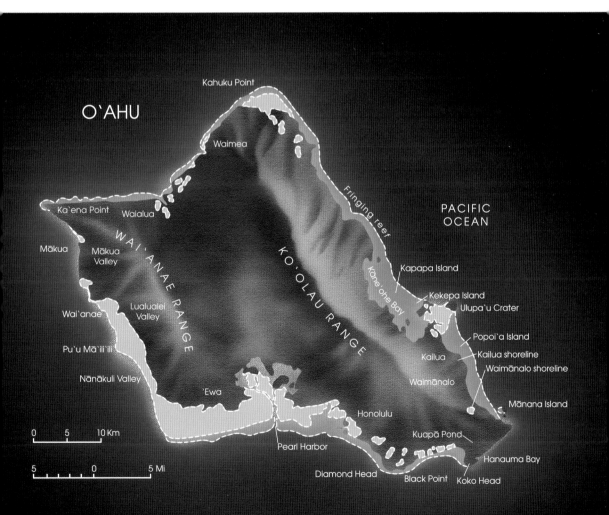

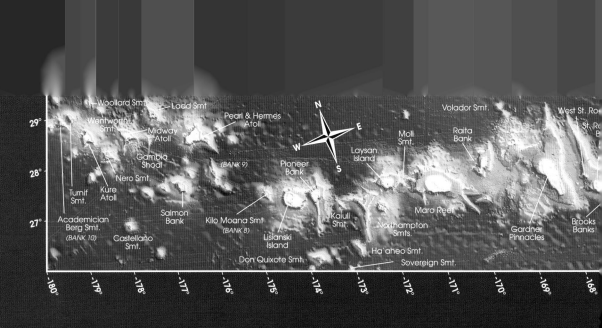

Figure 22 is a reproduction of the most detailed map of the Hawaiian Chain (Hawai'i Island to Kure Atoll) ever produced. The map was recently (2011) constructed by Dr. John R. Smith (Hawai'i Undersea Research Laboratory) and Dr. Paul Johnson (Hawai'i Mapping Research Group) at the University of Hawai'i. The map is a synthesis of bathymetric (depth) data collected by numerous sources over the years including the University of Hawai'i, the National Oceanic and Atmospheric Administration, the US Geological Survey and the National Science Foundation. The map includes data based on the latest technology using multibeam sonar. It covers over 1,400 miles of the Hawaiian Chain and includes 57 individual islands, seamounts, atolls, ridges and submerged land forms. Even so, it represents only about half of the entire Hawaiian-Emperor Archipelago. A map with equivalent detail of the drowned seamounts that constitute the more northern half of the Archipelago has yet to be produced.

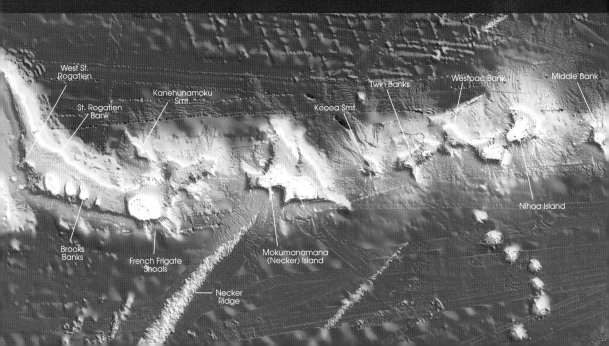

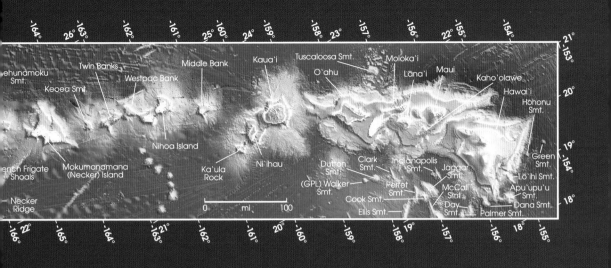

RELIEF IN METERS

ABOVE
FIGURE 22. Between the Big Island of Hawai'i and Kure Atoll, only seventeen islands exist above sea level. More than 97.5 percent of the archipelago's volume is underwater.

BELOW
FIGURE 23. Close-up detail of figure 22 showing the high islands and the lower Leewards.

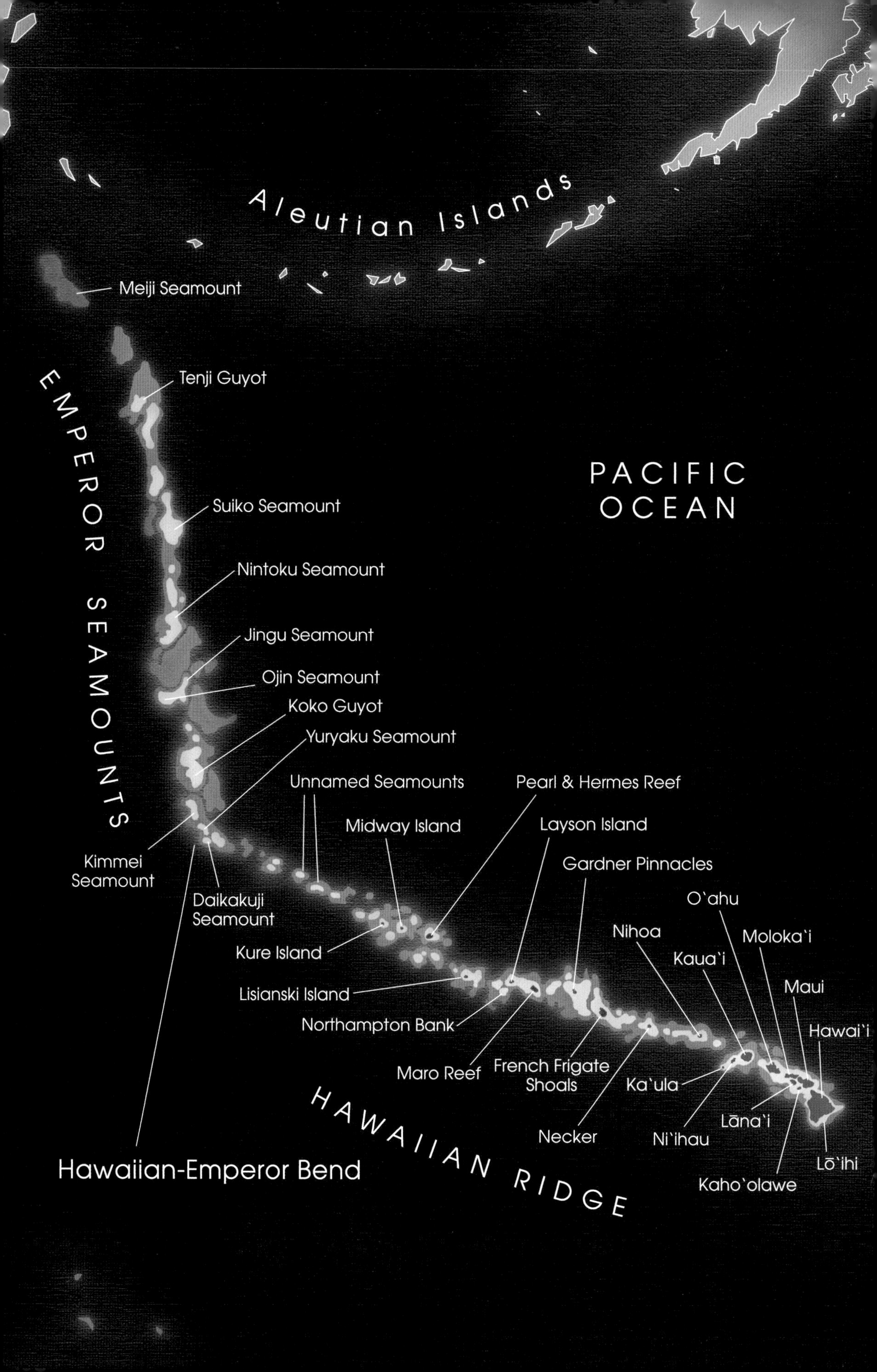

Aleutian Islands
Meiji Seamount
Tenji Guyot
EMPEROR SEAMOUNTS
PACIFIC OCEAN
Suiko Seamount
Nintoku Seamount
Jingu Seamount
Ojin Seamount
Koko Guyot
Yuryaku Seamount
Unnamed Seamounts
Pearl & Hermes Reef
Midway Island
Layson Island
Kimmei Seamount
Gardner Pinnacles
Daikakuji Seamount
O`ahu
Nihoa
Moloka`i
Kure Island
Kaua`i
Lisianski Island
Maui
Northampton Bank
Hawai`i
Maro Reef
French Frigate Shoals
Ka`ula
HAWAIIAN RIDGE
Lāna`i
Necker
Ni`ihau
Lō`ihi
Hawaiian-Emperor Bend
Kaho`olawe

CHAPTER 4

ARCHIPELAGO OF THE AGES

GEOGRAPHY

The Hawaiian Archipelago is the longest and oldest chain of islands on the face of the Earth. To fully appreciate its significance in space and time, it is necessary to backtrack chronologically and then sequentially reconstruct the chain beginning about seventy million years ago when Meiji Seamount was sitting directly over the Hawaiian hot spot. A map of the chain today (figure 24) shows that between approximately seventy million years and fifty million years ago, the Pacific Plate must have been moving over the Hawaiian hot spot in an almost due north direction. This section of about forty volcanoes represents the Emperor Seamounts. It is the upper limb or upper one-third of the chain. Interestingly, the Emperor Seamounts are almost all named after Japanese emperors (in honor of Dr. Risaburo Tayama, who first described them). Beginning with Meiji at the northern end of the chain and moving south, the major volcanic edifices are Tenji, Jimmu, Suiko, Yomei, Nintoku, Jingu, Ojin, Koko, Kimmei, Yuryaku, Daikakuji, and Kammu. The last five mark the southern end of the Emperors and are sometimes called the Milwaukee Seamounts. They are famous for the huge beds of valuable precious corals that are found there.

Several of the Emperor Seamount names are of particular interest. Jimmu for example, was the legendary first emperor of Japan, who ruled from 660 to 585 BC. Kammu was the fiftieth emperor of Japan, reigning from 782 to 805 AD. He was responsible for moving the capital of Japan to what is now Kyoto. Meiji was the reigning title of the 122nd emperor Mutsuhito, who is famous for having lifted feudal rule in Japan in 1867, allowing free enterprise to exist for the first time in Japanese history. The Meiji Reform is sometimes compared with Abraham Lincoln's Emancipation Proclamation in 1863 that, of course, freed the slaves in America.

FIGURE 24. Hawaiian volcanic and Emperor Seamount Chain. The lower limb dates from the present to about fifty million years ago; the upper leg north of the bend is approximately fifty million to seventy million plus years old.

The southern end of the Emperors is also of interest because it coincides with a dramatic change in the direction of plate motion over the Hawaiian hot spot shifting almost 60 degrees to the northwest (figure 24). Over the last fifty million years up to the present, the Pacific Plate must have been moving over the Hawaiian hot spot at a near constant speed (about three to four inches/eight to ten centimeters a year) and direction to the northwest. All the other seventy or so volcanoes in the chain were formed during this longer span of time. The cause of the bend is unknown, although as mentioned in chapter 3, some scientists have speculated that it may have been triggered by the collision of India with Eurasia, which possibly changed the torque on the Pacific Plate. Prior to collision, India was an island in the Indian Ocean drifting north on what then was the Indo-Australian Plate. It is also possible that the bend was caused by southerly drift of the hot spot itself during the first twenty million years of the Hawaiian Archipelago's history, although there is no physical mechanism to support this theory.

On the scale of the whole archipelago, one of the most interesting phenomena is that the hot spot seems to be getting more active. Compared to the Emperor Seamounts and the Northwestern Hawaiian Islands, the Main Hawaiian Islands are definitely the largest islands ever produced by the hot spot. In the past five million years, volcanic propagation has accelerated significantly to more than double the rate of earlier sections of the chain. With several exceptions (including Koko Seamount and Gardner Pinnacles) the MHI are significantly larger and closer together than their ancestors were.

In the next chapter, I describe the colonization of the islands over their entire history. But to understand the beginning years, it is useful to visualize the present L-shape of the archipelago and then turn it upside down. Instead of the present long leg to the northwest with an upper limb pointing north, we must imagine the islands first drifting almost straight north and then after about twenty million years bending to the northwest for the next fifty million years thus forming a backward and upside-down L. This is important for biology because it explains how the climate might have been colder for the first leg of volcanoes compared to the second limb of the island chain.

THE DARWIN POINT

Before examining the archipelago in further detail, it is important to consider how coral reefs have affected the history of the entire chain of islands, seamounts and guyots. This is the story of the Darwin Point. It is a story that actually began with Charles Darwin on April 12, 1836, during the expedition of the HMS Beagle. On that day, the ship had landed at Point Venus on the island of Tahiti in French Polynesia. That afternoon, the ship's famous naturalist, Charles Darwin, took a hike up the mountain behind Point Venus. When he reached an elevation of several hundred feet above sea level, he sat down to rest and peered out to the northwest. What he saw was the magnificent island of Moorea, so beautiful it is sometimes called the Bali Hai of the South Pacific. Moorea, then as now, is a high volcanic island surrounded by a coral barrier reef against which breaking waves create a lei of white water. Inside the reef is a still and tranquil shallow lagoon. That night Darwin made the following entry in his journal:

> Hence if we imagine such an island after long successive intervals, to subside a few feet in a manner similar to but with a movement opposite to the continent of South America; the coral would be continued upwards, rising from the foundation of the encircling reef. In time, the central land would sink beneath the level of the sea and disappear, but the coral would have completed its circular wall. Should we not then have a lagoon island? Under this view, we must look at a lagoon island as a monument raised by myriads of tiny architects to mark the spot where a former land lies buried in the depths of the ocean.

FIGURE 25. Diagrams illustrating Darwin's theory of atoll formation, which he published in his 1839 book on coral reefs.

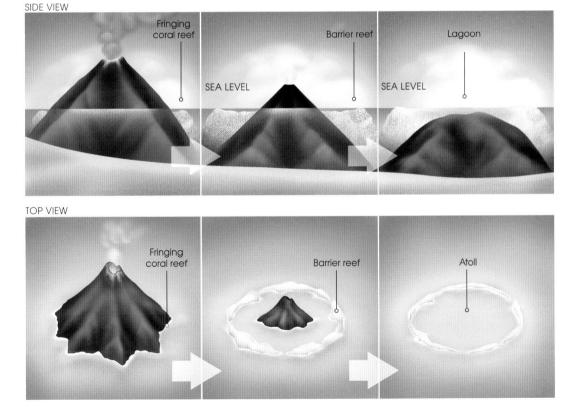

It would be 115 years later at Enewetak Atoll in the Marshall Islands in the north Pacific that Darwin's theory of atoll formation would finally be tested and confirmed. There in 1951, scientists drilled two cores deep into the rim of the atoll reef that descended 4,155 and 4,608 feet respectively before striking a volcanic rock basement. All the cores recovered were of shallow-water coral, proving that the upward growth of corals had taken place on the foundation of Enewetak volcano that had been subsiding for millions of years. The age of basement lava rock in the cores was estimated to be forty-nine million years. The upward growth of coral had only needed to be a fraction of an inch per year to keep pace with sea level above the sinking volcano. Charles Darwin's ability to imagine the vastness of time and the consequences of time was one of the secrets to his genius and, of course, was instrumental in his other famous theory, evolution by natural selection.

Just twenty years later, in 1971, I had just finished my graduate work at the Scripps Institution of Oceanography in La Jolla, California, and had been hired as a marine biologist at the University of Hawai'i. In that year, I would begin what would become a long-term study of coral growth rates in the Hawaiian Islands. The early 1970s was also about the same time that evidence was gathering in favor of seafloor spreading and John Tuzo Wilson's theory that the Hawaiian Islands were formed by the Earth's crust moving northwest over a fixed hot spot in the Earth's mantle. As mentioned in chapter 3, in 1972 Jason Morgan proposed that hot spots were produced by deep mantle plumes. The idea that the Hawaiian Islands were drifting to the northwest and slowly subsiding was taking hold and scientists were hard at work tracking individual islands dating their ages, erosion, and subsidence histories (table I).

TABLE I. AGE AND GEOGRAPHY OF THE MAIN HAWAIIAN ISLANDS					
ISLAND	AGE*	LATITUDE	ELEVATION TODAY†	MAX. ELEVATION†	SUBSIDENCE†
Big Island (Hawai'i)	0.5	19.5°N	13,792	15,088	~ 4,000
Maui	1.75	20.8°N	10,020	16,400	6,380
Kaho'olawe	1.75	20.5°N	1,476	6,888	5,412
Lāna'i	1.30	20.8°N	3,369	7,216	3,847
Moloka'i	1.75	21.1°N	4,969	10,824	5,855
O'ahu	3.7	21.5°N	4,038	7,216	3,178
Kaua'i	5.1	22.1°N	5,243	8,528	3,285
Ni'ihau	4.9	21.9°N	1,279	4,592	3,313

* in millions of years   † in feet

Note that all the islands "downstream" of the hot spot have subsided between roughly three thousand and six thousand feet since reaching maximum elevation over the hot spot.

TABLE II. AGE AND GEOGRAPHY OF THE NORTHWESTERN HAWAIIAN ISLANDS				
ISLAND	AGE*	LATITUDE	ELEVATION†	AREA‡
Nihoa	7.2	23.0°N	910	0.3
Necker	10.3	23.5°N	277	0.1
French Frigate Shoals	12.0	23.8°N	135	0.1
Gardner Pinnacles	12.3	25.0°N	190	~ 0.01
Laysan	19.9	25.8°N	35	1.5
Lisianski	23.4	26.0°N	20	0.7
Pearl and Hermes Atoll	26.8	27.8°N	10	0.1
Midway Islands	27.7	28.1°N	12	2.0
Kure	29.8	28.4°N	20	0.4
* in millions of years † in feet ‡ in square miles				

In the early 1970s, it was also known that all the NWHI were gradually sinking, albeit at a very slow rate. Furthermore, it was very clear that the last five islands in the Hawaiian Chain were all coral islands, probably resting atop the foundations of ancient volcanoes that long ago had subsided below sea level. That they had remained at sea level at all was an obvious testament to the validity of Darwin's original theory of atoll formation. To prove this idea, all that was needed was for someone to measure the upward rate of coral growth on every island in the Hawaiian Chain. I had been thinking about doing this for several years, but there was also the bigger question of how to do it.

In the meantime, I had been working on another coral reef study on the lava flows on the Big Island of Hawai'i. A volcanic eruption of Mauna Ulu in 1971 had sent rivers of lava from an elevation of four thousand feet over and down the mountain (pali) and into the ocean near 'Āpua Point, the easternmost tip of the Big Island. For several months, lava poured into the sea (figure 26) giving us an opportunity for the first time in history to actually dive, witness, and film this amazing spectacle underwater. It turned out to be truly spectacular.

Before describing what it looked like underwater, I must admit to the apprehension that we all felt. Was this idea safe, or was it crazy, or even doable? At the point of entry of the lava, the water would obviously be too hot to enter. We would have to scuba dive along the edge of the hot water plume hoping that we could swim down under it without being scalded. What happened was pretty lucky. After a couple of dives along the edge of the plume, we discovered that the hot water had formed a shallow lens of water about forty feet thick that was floating on cooler water below. It appeared that all we had to do was to dive down about fifty feet, stay below the hot layer, and hope that it wouldn't get any thicker before we reached the bottom where lava was cascading downslope.

LEFT
FIGURE 26.
Molten lava
hotter than
2000 degrees
Fahrenheit
entering the
sea at sea
level at ʻĀpua
Point, on the
east coast of
the Big Island,
in 1971.

BELOW
FIGURE 27.
A slab of lava
cracks open,
releasing heat
and pressure
from an
advancing
lava tube.

On our first dive to the bottom, I entered the water about one hundred yards offshore. It was outside the steaming plume of hot water that was clearly visible on the surface. My diving buddy was actually one of my students, Steve Dollar, and I said, "OK, Steve, you lead the way." With a scowl, Steve seemed to understand the choice. The water was clear, so we started down. We immediately could hear the crackling noise of the lava exploding underwater. When we got to a depth of about fifty feet, we headed directly for shore, kicking slowly and looking ahead and down. After several minutes, it started getting very dark. We were under the plume that was filled with thousands of bits of shattered lava not much larger than sand. Suddenly we began to see red cracks on the bottom. Then the bottom was moving and exploding as it moved. Pillows of lava opened up but instantly imploded shut. As we got closer we could see a twisting, ropy tangle of exploding volcanic debris winding downslope like a dying dragon (figure 27). The water was still relatively cool, but we could feel boils of hot water billowing up around us. We decided to collect a couple of samples, take a dozen or so quick pictures, and then get the hell out of there. And that is exactly what we did. By the end of that day, we had captured Pele as she looks underwater, almost as angry as she ever has looked on land. It was good to get that dive under our belts.

But our story here is about coral, not so much the active lava flow. In the next few years, we would discover the growth rates of various species of coral as well as the long-term growth of entire reefs growing on older and older lava flows dating back to 1801. We also found that there were major species of coral that had annual growth rings just like trees. As it turned out, the most important reef-building species of coral was a massive lobe-shaped form called *Porites lobata*, and it had very clear annual growth rings (see figure 28). It was also significant that its growth rate was intermediate (average) among all the common Hawaiian reef corals. Because of this fact and its dominant importance in building the solid structure of the reef, its growth rate could be used as an average, or proxy, for all the other species of coral on the reef.

At once, the idea of measuring the rate of coral reef growth on every island in the chain seemed doable. We could simply measure the living coral cover of all species at stations of optimal depth and ecology off every island in the chain and apply a station-specific growth rate based on collected colonies of *Porites lobata*. If ten colonies of *Porites lobata* at least ten years old could be collected at each island station, the growth ring data produced would be based on at least one hundred years of data. This growth rate could be multiplied by the average coral cover of all species present to produce estimates of the upward growth of the entire reef for each island station.

Given the feasibility of actually conducting such a project, it would not be long before I began writing a research proposal to obtain the funding, titled Project Darwin Point. The basic idea was to provide another test of Darwin's theory for the origin of coral atolls. Another important reason for measuring the upward growth rate of coral reefs on every island in the chain was to see if it would explain why the archipelago above sea level ended at Kure Atoll. In other words, did the islands that drifted north of Kure Atoll due to plate movement drown because the coral stopped growing? If so, many of the seamounts that now exist northwest of Kure Atoll are really drowned atolls, also known as guyots. The actual point of drowning could be called the Darwin Point. It would represent a latitudinal threshold beyond which atolls could not remain above sea level.

There would be no doubt that such an experiment would be of great scientific interest, but getting the research funding is sometimes more difficult than the work itself. However, as luck would have it, it turned out to be a perfect time to propose such a project. In March of 1977, the United States extended its jurisdiction over its ocean boundaries from twelve to two hundred miles. Almost overnight, a large pot of research funding was appropriated by the US Congress to assess all the ocean resources in this vast new ocean space. It was called EJ money, for extended jurisdiction in the territorial sea. I took the Darwin Point Project, joined forces with four agencies—the state of Hawai'i, the US Sea Grant College Program, the National Marine Fisheries Service, and the US Fish and Wildlife Service—and proposed a five-year study of the Northwestern Hawaiian Islands. As a collective effort, the entire program was funded. Along with corals, the program studied basic oceanography, plankton production, shallow- and deep-reef fisheries, offshore migratory fisheries, lobsters, green turtles, monk seals, and even marine birds. And for the coral project, the timing and duration of the program was very fortunate indeed, since it took five years to collect the data.

About one hundred people from fishermen to university researchers to graduate students took part in the program. We visited every island and shallow bank in the entire archipelago many times over and in some cases even lived on an island for weeks at a time. An encyclopedia of information was collected over the next five years, two scientific symposia were held, and more than one hundred scientific research papers were published. Management plans for green turtles and monk seals were created, as well as, were Fishery Management Plans for lobsters, bottom fish, pelagic fish, and precious corals.

In 1982 I published a paper entitled "The Darwin Point: A Threshold for Atoll Formation" in the science journal Coral Reefs. Basically, the growth-rate data that we collected for *Porites lobata* and whole reefs from the Big Island of Hawai'i all the way up the chain to Kure Atoll showed that coral growth steadily declined from about 0.5 inches (13 millimeters) a year at the southeastern end of the chain to nearly zero growth just beyond Kure Atoll (figure 29).

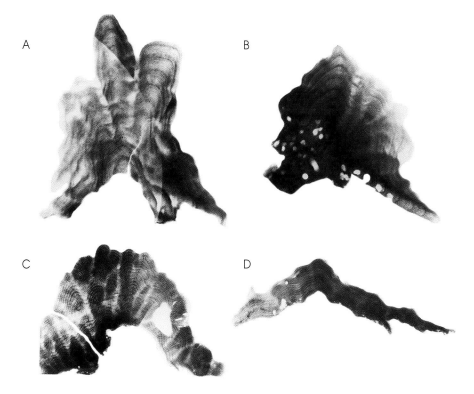

FIGURE 28. Annual growth rings in *Porites lobata* in four colonies collected off (A) The Big Island, (B) French Frigate Shoals, (C) Pearl and Hermes Atoll, and (D) Kure Atoll. Note the dramatic decrease in coral growth rate (thickness of the annual growth rings) at locations further north in the Hawaiian Chain.

Therefore, any island that drifted northwest of Kure Atoll would slowly drown. The causal factors are decreasing temperature and sunlight as latitude increases moving up the chain. The average annual temperature beyond Kure Atoll is too low for coral to survive, and sunlight is insufficient to support the symbiotic algae living inside the corals. The threshold for drowning is called the Darwin Point.

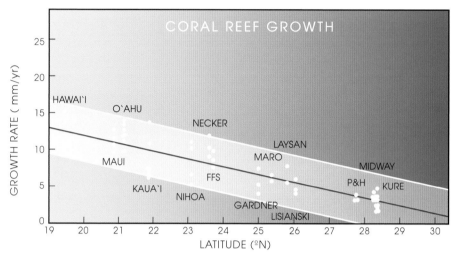

FIGURE 29. Growth rate of *Porites lobata* plotted as a function of increasing latitude in the Hawaiian Chain from the Big Island to Kure. Note that reef accretion (upward growth) reaches zero at a latitude just beyond Kure Atoll.

Hence, once a coral reef (or coral island) was (or is) transported beyond the Darwin Point, corals would stop growing, and the island would slowly drown (figure 30). The experiment once again confirmed Darwin's theory of atoll formation and produced a minimum or threshold value for coral growth necessary for a coral island to remain at sea level. Thus, without coral growth, the Hawaiian Archipelago would be about half its present length, drowning at the point where the last volcanic peak would sink below the waves. Today this would be Gardner Pinnacles. Laysan, Lisianski, Pearl and Hermes Atoll, Midway Islands, and Kure Atoll would not exist at sea level were it not for the upward growth of their coral reefs. Instead, they would be drowned seamounts or guyots just like all the rest of the Emperor Seamounts today.

THE NORTHWESTERN HAWAIIAN ISLANDS AND THE EMPEROR SEAMOUNTS

Before our voyage revisits the Emperor Seamounts, there is much more that should be said about the NWHI. In time and space, these islands occupy about twenty million years and about twelve hundred miles of the archipelago, 30 percent of its total age and length. Table II (page 41) charts the ages and geographic aspects of each major NWHI. Today, Nihoa, Necker, and Gardner Pinnacles are low rocky islets; French Frigate Shoals is a virtual atoll (with two

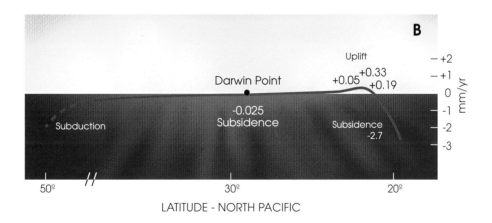

Zone 4

Subduction in
Kamchatka
Trench

Zone 3

Reef coral growth
ceases, continued
subsidence, atolls
drown to form guyots.

Zone 2

Barrier reef
become atolls,
continued
subsidence

Zone 1

Subaerial erosion,
subsidence,
fringing and
barrier reefs.

A

Darwin Point

54º N
163º E

29º N

24º N

19º N
155º W

SEA LEVEL

EAST
PACIFIC
RISE

KAMCHATKA

46

28

11.7

5.6

0.8

PACIFIC LITHOSPHERIC PLATE

Subduction

ASTHENOSPHERE

MELTING
ANOMALY
OR "HOT SPOT"

B

Uplift

Darwin Point

+0.05 +0.33
+0.19

−0.025
Subsidence

Subsidence
-2.7

+2
+1
0
−1
−2
−3

mm/yr

Subduction

50º

30º

20º

LATITUDE - NORTH PACIFIC

FIGURE 30. (A) Depiction of the entire history of the Hawaiian Archipelago. (B) The islands first undergo rapid building, then rapid subsidence, followed by a small wrinkle of uplift, then continued subsidence at a much slower but continuous rate due to the cooling of the Pacific Plate, and finally subduction into the Kamchatka Trench. The whole cycle requires more than seventy million years from island birth to death.

small emergent volcanic pinnacles); Laysan and Lisianski are coral islands with no lagoons; and Pearl and Hermes, Midway, and Kure are true atolls with well-established lagoons surrounded by barrier reefs (figures 31-33).

Except for the rocky islets and pinnacles mentioned above, all the NWHI are nearly flat, low-lying structures existing just a few feet above sea level and consisting of primarily sand and reef deposits. Deposits of guano once existed on Laysan and Lisianski but were mined to near depletion near the turn of the twentieth century (see chapter 6).

The information in table II (page 41) represents the present time, what might be called the modern period. However, just twenty-one thousand years ago at the peak of the last ice age, sea level was about four hundred feet lower than it is today. Back then, the NWHI would have all been about four hundred feet higher. They might have looked like minicastles of limestone uplifted in the sea or perhaps like shipwrecked aircraft carriers resting on shallow shoals. Looking further back in time, millions of years ago the NWHI were once much larger high islands. This was when they were much younger and closer to their site of origin over the hot spot.

Today, the importance of the NWHI goes well beyond their miniscule area, particularly when you consider the huge shallow-water wave-cut shelves (less than two hundred feet deep) that encircle so many of them. Nihoa, Necker, Gardner Pinnacles, Laysan, and Lisianski would be at least one hundred times larger if the area of their shelves were to be exposed—as they would be during periods of lower sea-level. The NWHI are also important due to their biological connectivity both in shallow and deep water to the MHI and the Emperor Seamounts.

The atolls near the end of the chain (see table II) are also significant because their underlying reefs contain a historical archive of the geological history of the Hawaiian Chain. Being the northernmost and oldest members of the emergent chain, their subsurface layered stratigraphy holds a chronological record that goes back to their time of origin over the hot spot. For this reason, the US Geological Survey and the Smithsonian Institution drilled two deep cores in the reef at Midway Islands. The cores were of sufficient depth to reach the basalt foundation of the atoll. Midway Islands are just sixty miles southeast of Kure Atoll, the end of the archipelago at 28.4 degrees north. The location of both atolls approximates the position of the Darwin Point beyond which coral islands drown. As such, Kure and Midway mark the end of the subaerial (above sea-level) Hawaiian Islands.

With support from the National Science Foundation, the two deep cores were drilled in the summer of 1965. The first core hole was drilled on Sand Island, the major islet on Midway and the site of an airport and many buildings constructed before and during World War II. This core reached basalt at a depth

FIGURE 31.
Necker Island is one of three islets in the Northwestern Hawaiian Islands. The other two are Nihoa and Gardner Pinnacles.

FIGURE 32.
French Frigate Shoals is a near-atoll with only two tiny remnants of basalt (including the rocky outcrop La Perouse Pinnacle) of what was formerly a very large high island.

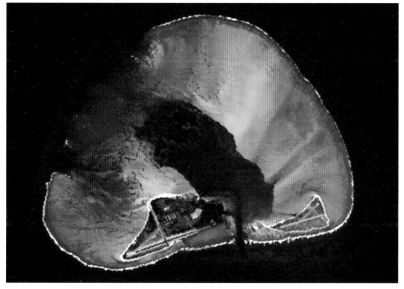

FIGURE 33.
Midway Islands are famous for battles, biology, and birds.

of 516 feet and continued down to 568 feet. The second core was located just inside the northern edge of the atoll reef; it entered basalt at 1,261 feet and was continued to 1,654 feet. Radiometric dating of the oldest basalts recovered from both cores produced an age of about twenty-eight million years for the island. From this data, the subsidence rate of the atoll could be calculated, which turned out to be very slow overall but also very steady at approximately 0.0008 inches (0.02 millimeters) a year. The cores also revealed that Midway Islands apparently underwent two or three periods of emergence above sea level and then resubmergence, probably as a result of glacial-interglacial episodes of rising and falling sea level. All the other Hawaiian Islands would have been exposed to the same oscillations of sea level. Interestingly, should the pacemaker of the ice ages continue into the future, not only will Oʻahu, and all its hotels in Waikīkī, someday drown, but they could also possibly reemerge as fossil castles in the sea before finally succumbing to an ocean tomb and final subduction.

Another very interesting discovery in the Midway cores was the pattern of extinction and recolonization of many coral reef species (fossils) that overlie the basalt foundation of the island. At the bottom of the core, there was a group of corals that lasted about five million years. This community was then replaced by an entirely different mix that in turn persisted for another five to eight million years. This period was followed by a gap of several million years with no corals at all. It may have been a time of rising sea level that caused Midway to temporarily drown, pushing the Darwin Point south into warmer waters. After the gap, there was another period of recolonization, during which time a last group of coral species became established, and in fact, are still present in the island chain. If most other species behave like corals do, what this means is that the norm is not ecological constancy. Instead, the norm appears to be change, albeit over very long periods of time.

Moving north once again, table III tabulates the ages, depths, summit areas, and ancient sea level history of the Emperor Seamounts. What is most interesting is that six or eight of the seamounts were once elevated islands, high above sea level. That was millions of years ago when they were located at a more southerly and warmer latitude.

Koko Guyot in particular must have rivaled the size of the Big Island of Hawaiʻi. Koko Guyot today has a summit area of more than two thousand square miles and a summit depth of only 850 feet. Back calculation of the location and time that Koko Guyot must have drowned (using a subsidence rate of 0.0008 inches/0.02 millimeters a year) puts its point of submergence at about 32 degrees north. This is only about 2 degrees north of the present-day estimate of the latitude of the Darwin Point. Moreover, since we know the radiometric age of Koko Guyot is about fifty million years, this would mean that it was above sea level for about thirty-five million years of its history. In the next chapter, we will investigate the question of what might have lived there during those

TABLE III. AGE AND GEOGRAPHY OF THE EMPEROR SEAMOUNTS					
SEAMOUNT	AGE*	LATITUDE	DEPTH†	SUMMIT AREA‡	SEA LEVEL HISTORY
Daikakuji	46.7	32°N	3,250	200	seamount
Kammu	43	32°N	1,100	290	seamount
Yuryaku	50	33°N	1,570	150	seamount
Kimmei	47.9	34°N	1,340	290	seamount
Koko	52.6	35°N	850	2,250	elevated
Jingu	47–55	39°N	2,650	500	seamount
Nintoku	56	41°N	3,300	1,300	elevated
Yomei	?	42°N	3,000	780	seamount
Suiko	58–64	44°N	3,100	1,270	elevated
Jimmu	?	46°N	4,100	320	seamount
Tenji	?	49°N	6,240	350	seamount
Detroit	?	51°N	7,160	2,700	tablemount
Meiji	72	53°N	9,350	3,200	elevated
* in millions of years † in feet ‡ in square miles					

ancient times. Several of the other large Emperor Seamounts must have experienced a history similar to that of Koko.

Many other seamounts in the Emperor Chain may have been elevated for several million years (see table III). Based on their present-day summit areas, radiometric ages, and subsidence rates, Meiji, Detroit, and Suiko Seamounts may have been very large islands. In contrast, toward the southern end of the Emperor Chain, the volcanoes are much smaller and may never have been emergent, remaining seamounts throughout their entire lives. However, in either case, all the Emperors would have always supported a deep-sea fauna belonging to many different taxonomic groups, including fish, sponges, deep-sea corals, and a myriad of invertebrates (animals without backbones).

The Emperor Seamounts, and all the islands in the Hawaiian Archipelago, will eventually share the present-day fate of Meiji, which is now undergoing gradual subduction into the Aleutian–Kamchatka Trench. Having been born a fiery volcano some seventy million–plus years ago, Meiji will return to its origins, to remelt back into the mantle. While the Hawaiian Archipelago is the greatest island chain on Earth, it is also a great conveyor belt of island life to death: fire to fire, dust to dust. Some twenty-five other hot spots that exist on planet Earth have produced similar and ever-changing cycles of island archipelagos or volcanic chains. The Earth is as restless as is the universe. It is a constantly fluctuating voyage across space and time. As passengers, we can only observe in wonder and be in awe of this great cosmic dance.

CHAPTER 5

LIFE ON THE ISLAND ARKS

LIFE DISCOVERS HAWAI'I

The story of life in Hawai'i must begin with Meiji, the first island that erupted through the skin of the north Pacific Ocean about seventy million–plus years ago. In chapter 1 we learned that Meiji is now on the brink of destruction, on the edge of the Aleutian-Kamchatka Trench where soon (geologically speaking) it will be pushed and pulled down back into the Earth from whence it came, to remelt within the mantle. But seventy million years ago, it was a volcano just emerging over the Hawaiian hot spot. There could even have been younger islands that preceded Meiji, but if so, they would have already subducted and would be long gone. So we must begin with Meiji soon after it broke the surface of the ocean and could support life.

What kind of ocean world surrounded Meiji seventy million years ago? It was the end of the Mesozoic era, a time when dinosaurs were running amuck in the jungles of the continents and great white sharks more than forty feet long and many other heavily jawed fishes roamed the seas (figure 34). It was before the famous Cretaceous-Tertiary (abbreviated K-T) asteroid slammed into the Earth on the Yucatán Peninsula in Mexico sixty-five million years ago (figure 35), wiping out up to 70 percent of the world's species, which up till then were happily thriving, albeit subject to the laws of the tooth and claw.

The ocean and the continents were also much different seventy million years ago. North and South America were not connected, nor was the Indonesian seaway filled with islands (Philippines, Celebes, Indonesia, Borneo, etc.) as it is today. The great Gulf Stream in the Atlantic, the Kuroshio Current in the northwestern Pacific, and the North Pacific Drift were all very weak if not altogether nonexistent. At the equator, the currents were like a continuous

FIGURE 34. Dinosaur-like fishes roamed the seas about the same time the first Hawaiian Island was born over seventy million years ago.

FIGURE 35. Artist's rendering of the K-T extinction event, an asteroid that hit the Earth about sixty-five million years ago and wiped out huge numbers of species on land and in the sea.

belt that went all the way around the Earth, mostly east to west, nourished by converging trade winds. In this ancient time, the average climate of the world was warmer than it is today. It was a greenhouse world, and the continents were verdant, lush, and full of life.

In the very beginning, however, Meiji Island must have been a very desolate place. By itself, the island would have been one of the most isolated places on Earth. Born in the middle of the Pacific, the largest of the oceans, Meiji was literally in the middle of nowhere. At first, there would have been just hot sterile rock and superheated steam, exploding lava as it hit the sea, ash, cinder, crashing waves, wind, and gale. The sun was so intense and the black lava surfaces so hot that rain would have evaporated in seconds. Even though many open-ocean organisms must have been swirling around the island, it would take hundreds if not thousands of years before spores and insects in the wind, seeds in the feathers of birds, and larvae in the drifting waters would take foothold on the island foundations and begin reproducing life-building populations and communities. Of course, all this would have been long before Madam Pele blessed her islands.

With the gathering of life around Meiji, the great conveyor belt of time began to turn, and the hot spot would produce many more islands and seamounts. The next volcano to erupt would be Detroit, then Tenji, Jimmu, and Suiko, followed by Yomei, Nintoku, and Jingu, then Ojin, Koko, and Kimmei, and many of these volcanoes would be elevated above sea level (see table III, page 51). The first segment of islands was carried almost straight north by the Pacific Plate, and therefore these islands would have drifted into slightly cooler water. Completion of the Emperors took about thirty-five million–plus years, the NWHI another thirty million–plus years, and the Main High Hawaiian Islands a final five million–plus years (see figure 2, page 7). Throughout this entire span of time, the archipelago would continue to be relatively isolated from source areas such as the Indo-West Pacific (IWP) biogeographic region. All the islands would have been between two thousand to five thousand miles distant from the nearest continent and perhaps one thousand miles from the nearest island. Hence, the diversity of the Hawaiian flora and fauna (biota) would always remain low compared to source areas around the Pacific.

But as time passed, erosion would till the land, and water would carve streams and rivers. Ponds and low-lying wetlands would form. Waves would shear back volcanic cliffs into flat shallow shorelines and reefs. More time passed, not just years, but millions of them, and terrestrial seeds and spores and marine larvae would arrive (figure 36), as well as full-fledged gravid adults ready to give birth to their spawn. Adult birds would fly in from all directions. Sometimes, huge rafts of broken trees and other flotsam full of hitchhikers would wash up on Hawaiian shores, having been carried across the Pacific by currents from the IWP and even from North America. Gradually, flora and fauna would build island arks: communities of all kinds, living in forests, high-elevation swamps, lowland marshes, jungles, sand and strand habitats, rocky intertidal areas, on reefs, in canyons, on deep shelves and abyssal plains, and of course in the seawater itself, free of any attachment to the bottom.

To approximate what might have existed during the early millennia of the archipelago, it is perhaps useful to jump ahead to nearly the present day and briefly glimpse the major groups of organisms that existed in Hawai'i before contact by both the Hawaiians and the European explorers. At least ten thousand native species existed on land and more than two-thirds that many may have lived in the sea. It should be understood that species are populations of individuals that are reproductively isolated from other species. Different species simply do not mate together successfully, except for a very few exceptions. Closely related groups of species are cataloged into genera. Similar genera are organized into families, families into orders, orders into classes, and classes into phyla.

What major groups of native species are believed to have existed in Hawai'i before human contact? An estimate would include about 700 species of fungi; 260 mosses; 170 ferns; 1,000 flowering plants; 500 marine plants; 57 reef-building corals and 685 fish; 1,000 land snails; 1,500 marine mollusks; 5,000 marine

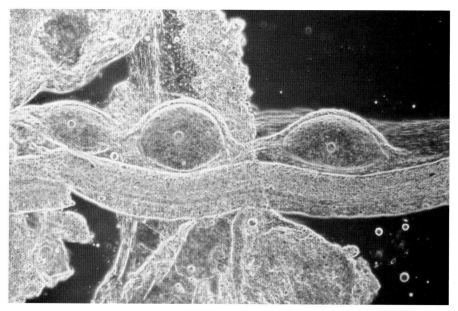

FIGURE 36. Coral eggs are expelled into the overlying water where they are fertilized and drift until they settle back to the bottom to resume growth into a new coral colony.

invertebrates; more than 100 birds; more than 6,000 insects and arthropods (crabs, shrimp, lobsters, spiders, tics, flies, etc.); 3 reptiles (turtles); 3 mammals (two bats and a monk seal); and several thousand other open-ocean or deep-water species that are not directly dependent on the islands. In all likelihood, far fewer organisms probably existed in the archipelago during its infancy and middle years, but there is almost no record except for tiny marine fossils that have been retrieved from deep-sea dredge hauls and drilling operations in the Emperor Seamounts and deep-reef cores collected from Midway Islands and the island of Oʻahu. Lacking any other direct records of ancient life in Hawaiʻi, it is necessary to consider what can be learned from this collective archive.

THE FOSSIL RECORD

Unfortunately, nothing definite can be said about Hawaiʻi's very ancient terrestrial life except that time has swept it away. Nevertheless, we can imagine what might have happened during those early millions of years, since there must have been major disturbance events. The K-T asteroid impact is known to have jolted life everywhere in the world about sixty-five million years ago. Coral reefs almost completely disappeared from the fossil record everywhere in the ocean, even in the IWP, and it would take ten or more million years for new species to reappear. Other cataclysmic events would also be commonplace in Hawaiʻi. Numerous volcanic eruptions, hurricanes, episodes of huge waves, landslides both above and below sea level, significant changes in sea level, earthquakes, and of course thousands of biological interactions of both short- and long-term significance must have occurred. Hawai'i has always been a very dynamic natural environment, and species extinction and recolonization events would be expected.

What little that can be said about early marine life in Hawai'i is based primarily on the fossil record obtained from the dredge hauls and cores from the Midway Islands (see page 48) and the Emperor Seamounts. Interestingly, all these samples were collected between 1965 and 1977 during a flurry of scientific exploration sponsored by the Smithsonian Institution and the US Deep Sea Drilling Program. As it turns out, the youngest corals found in any of these samples are from Koko Guyot and are dated at thirty-four million years, indicating that coral reefs were absent in the archipelago for the first half of its existence, for about thirty-five million years. The samples from the guyots and seamounts north of Koko are all dominated by algae and moss animals (Bryozoa), suggesting that climatic conditions there were cooler and more subtropical. Coral reefs, of course, are excellent indicators of climate conditions since they can normally only thrive in water temperatures between about 72 and 86 degrees Fahrenheit.

Another very interesting pattern revealed in the Midway cores, as mentioned in chapter 4, are the cycles of extinction and recolonization of reef corals with a turnover time of about five million years. It is also intriguing that the last species group may have persisted for about this length of time up until the present. John Wells of Cornell University, who dated all the Midway corals, describes the upper four hundred feet of the core as all post-Miocene, meaning that all the fossils are younger than five million years. The importance of this finding is that this pattern might also apply to all the coral reefs throughout the archipelago. Today, for example, the composition of coral reef communities is more or less similar throughout the MHI and NWHI. A small spike in abundance is found in the middle of the chain around French Frigate Shoals (figure 37), and there is a small decrease in species diversity at the end of the chain, but other than these somewhat minor differences, the species composition and community structure of coral reefs can be described as sharing a common membership. If true, what this means is that the age of the present-day marine fauna that exists in Hawai'i is no older than about five million years. On land, as we will see, terrestrial communities may be even younger. To clarify the meaning of age, particularly as used in this chapter, we are mainly referring to the age of a given species when it evolved. The larger taxonomic groupings of genera, family, order, class, and phylum would be expected to be progressively older, some going back many millions of years, as well as arising from virtually all corners of the world. Origin at these levels is beyond the scope of this book.

This does not mean that some genetic remnants of species older than five million years do not exist on the land or in the ocean around the Hawaiian Islands. Perhaps the best example of an older lineage in Hawai'i is a refuge of nine ancestral relicts of upland and mountain plants and animals that have

FIGURE 37. Reef corals in the Hawaiian Islands, such as French Frigate Shoals, are entirely IWP in origin, however, only 10 percent of the species that exist in the IWP also occur in Hawaiʻi.

been recently described from Laysan in the NWHI. Laysan is now a flat coral island a little south of Midway (figure 38), but about nineteen million years ago it was a high island located near or over the Hawaiian hot spot. Most of the nine relict lineages on Laysan, including several palms and trees, two birds, and a land snail, are now extinct, but their fossil remains prove that they lived there up until the 1800s, before major human disturbance events upset the island ecology. While these the dead remnants represent a very small percent of precontact life on Laysan, they demonstrate that at least some of the NWHI could have served as genetic sources for modern-day species. As to the possibility of earlier roots between modern life in Hawaiʻi and even older islands or the ancient Emperors, the distance in space and time between them make this unlikely. Given known rates of island sinking, the last Emperor "island" to drown was Koko Guyot. That was about thirteen million years ago, and Koko would have been almost one thousand miles northwest of the closest other elevated island (Midway or Kure). Connections would not have been impossible, but the chance of Emperor propagules from the land seeding the younger islands, or back-stepping down the chain, would have been unlikely.

Another way to understand the history of life in the archipelago is to look at rates of biological evolution. How long does it take for new species to form? To explain this, it is necessary to introduce and define several new terms. First, native species can be either indigenous or endemic. Indigenous species are naturally occurring but also exist in many other places in the world. Endemic species are forms that have evolved in Hawaiʻi and are found nowhere else. Species introduced by humans are called alien or exotic species and are described in

FIGURE 38. Laysan Island is an ancient atoll where the former lagoon has been filled in with wave-washed sand and coral rubble and is now a hypersaline lake.

chapter 6. The species diversity of both the land and marine biota in Hawai'i is severely depleted due to their common isolation from source areas of colonization. The term biologists apply to this condition is *disharmonic*, meaning that the biota is undersaturated. In other words, many more species could exist in Hawai'i were they able to get here. This is one reason why introduced species in Hawai'i often are extremely successful although not necessarily beneficial.

Differences between Life on the Land and in the Sea

The rate at which species evolve is not the same on land and in the sea. In fact, there are many fundamental differences between the two life realms. Temperature differences and gradients of other physical variables are much greater on land than in the sea. Also, on the land there is much greater habitat diversity, much more complexity, and many more kinds of places to live, or ecological niches. In the sea, there are fewer habitats, and they are very broadly spaced. On land, species are often highly specialized, living in microclimates, whereas in the sea marine forms are more generalized, living in very large areas. Using coral reefs as an example, coral communities on all the islands are much more similar to each other than land communities at comparable latitudes. Because of these many differences, evolution of new species by natural selection (survival of the most fit) and adaptive radiation on land is faster than it is in the sea. As one consequence of this, about 90 percent of many species groups on land are endemic to Hawaiʻi, compared to only about 25 to 30 percent in surrounding shallow marine communities. The average number of species per genus on land is about ten times greater than it is in the sea.

The differences between land and sea life in Hawaiʻi might best be illustrated by discussing several examples. On land, plants, fruit flies, and birds provide particularly interesting stories of rapid evolution and adaptive radiation. In the MHI there is a group of tarweed plants (sunflower relatives) known as the silversword alliance that contains twenty-eight species, all endemic, all very different in appearance, and all inhabiting a wide variety of habitats from the driest and highest mountains to the wettest forests and bogs. All twenty-eight species are thought to have evolved in just two million years from the seeds of a single sunflower founder from California. The flowering of one silversword species that grows in the cloud forests of Maui and Hawaiʻi is incredibly spectacular. After thirty years of growth, forming plants up to ten feet tall, a single massive stalk grows out of the heart of the plant and produces up to five hundred yellow to red-brown flowers (figure 40). After this single burst of reproductive exuberance, the plant dies.

Fruit flies of the genus *Drosophila* (figure 39) provide an even more spectacular example of what is known as the founder effect. Founders are individuals or a small group of individuals (seeds, spores, larvae, or gravid adults) belonging to the same species that colonize a new geographic area and give rise to an emergent population. In the case where colonization is limited to a few founders, the genetic variety within the population may be very limited, giving rise to something called genetic drift. Genetic drift occurs when natural selection in the founder population only has a few genes from which to "choose," leading to fewer ways to adapt to new or changing environmental conditions.

LEFT
FIGURE 39. One of the many species of fruit fly that live in Hawaiʻi.

RIGHT
FIGURE 40. The Hawaiian silversword in full flower.

About five hundred species of *Drosophila* have been scientifically described, and another three hundred are thought to exist in the high Hawaiian Islands. Many species occupy a single valley on a single island and hence are highly specialized in extremely narrow niches. It turns out that all eight hundred species are believed to have originated from one, or at most, two founding individuals that arrived in Hawai'i about five million years ago. Interestingly, the antiquity of the Hawaiian fruit fly can be roughly determined because the mutation rate in its salivary glands is known. Because of this, at least in annuls of science, *Drosophila* may be the world's most famous insect. In Hawai'i, of course, mosquitoes and cockroaches may be better known.

A third and well-known example of rapid speciation and adaptive radiation on the land in Hawai'i is found in the Hawaiian honeycreepers, a group of finchlike birds. Forty-seven species (twenty-four living and twenty-three extinct) are known to have evolved in Hawai'i, all arising from a single founder probably from North America about 3.5 million years ago (figure 41).

In the Galápagos Islands, Charles Darwin had only fourteen species of finches existing on fifteen separate islands to study. Their isolation from each other and the adaptation of their bills to different feeding habitats convinced Darwin that species are not fixed and unchangeable but instead slowly evolve (change) over long periods of time to originate into new species. Interestingly, like the Hawaiian honeycreepers, all fourteen species of finches in the Galápagos can be traced to a common ancestor from the mainland, in this case, South America. Had Darwin landed in Hawai'i instead of the Galápagos Islands, his "Garden of Eden" would have been even richer. Darwin may have instinctively known this since he once offered a reward of fifty pounds to any collector who would work in the Hawaiian Islands. Indeed, the land biota of Hawai'i is certainly one of the most extraordinary living museums of evolution that exists on the planet.

The claim of evolutionary uniqueness, however, may not apply as well to Hawai'i's shallow-water marine flora and fauna. We have seen that the rate of endemism in Hawai'i's marine flora and fauna is only 25 to 30 percent on average compared to 90 percent or more for many species groups on land. Why? Recalling the fundamental differences between each biosphere mentioned above, Hawai'i's marine world is not nearly as diverse as its lands. Marine species are more often generalized, occupying very broad niches. Indigenous marine species are open to constant recolonization and infusion from planktonic larvae that come in from outside the islands. Therefore the genetic makeup of various Hawaiian marine indigenous populations is constantly diluted by the addition of new genes. Rates of evolutionary change in such forms are therefore relatively slow. We have already seen in the Midway core that coral reefs there may not have changed over the last five million years. Quite logically then, if rates

FIGURE 41. Bill size and shape separates many species of honeycreepers in Hawai'i.

of larval colonization of a marine species to the islands is greater than its rate of speciation, then the gene pool of the species would be swamped and fewer endemic species would evolve.

The 90 to 99 percent incidence of endemism of many species groups on land must mean that speciation rates on land must be just the opposite of marine species. On land, speciation rates must be much faster than rates of immigration. When new colonists arrive on land, they must join populations that have already evolved into new species, and therefore no genetic exchange can occur. Land species in Hawai'i are much more isolated than those in the sea. What this also means is that the average evolutionary age of the land flora and fauna is much younger than it is in the sea, probably by several million years. The youngest species in both biological realms would be those with the highest rates of evolutionary change. This very powerful conclusion brings the questions of source area and colonization frequency back to the forefront.

BIOGEOGRAPHIC ORIGINS OF LIFE IN HAWAI'I

Overall, the many sources of Hawai'i's native biota represent a biogeographic tangle with many threads. But it is also true that life on the land and the sea in Hawai'i has always been dominated by immigration via the Indo-West-Pacific (IWP), if not directly, then by way of stepping stones of intervening islands or seamounts. Why this is so involves two major factors. First, the IWP is the richest source of biotic diversity in the world; it is the true Garden of Eden. Second, most pathways to Hawai'i come from the south, southwest, or the west. The IWP consists of all of the islands in Southeast Asia—the Philippine and Indonesian archipelagos, Borneo, the Celebes, and Papua New Guinea. Over evolutionary time, the IWP has been both a center of origin of species and a center of accumulation of species. Origin is common there because so many of its islands are isolated from each other, especially during the ice ages when sea level dropped about four hundred feet. The IWP is also an accumulation area for species that evolve out in the Pacific and then drift back to the west in surface currents near the equator. As for pathways to Hawai'i, it is necessary to look for currents and winds that are farther north and move to the east.

If we return to Hawai'i and look in both directions, to the west and to the east, we find large and important differences. To the east there are no islands that could have served as stepping stones for either life in the sea or on the land. Even underwater, there are few large seamounts between Hawai'i and the Americas. The gap separating them is basically several thousand miles of deep ocean water. To the west, especially the southwest, the ocean is littered with islands and underwater stepping stones (figure 42). As many as ten thousand seamounts have been estimated to exist in the Pacific Ocean, and the majority is found in a wide arc ranging from northwest to almost straight south of the Hawaiian Archipelago.

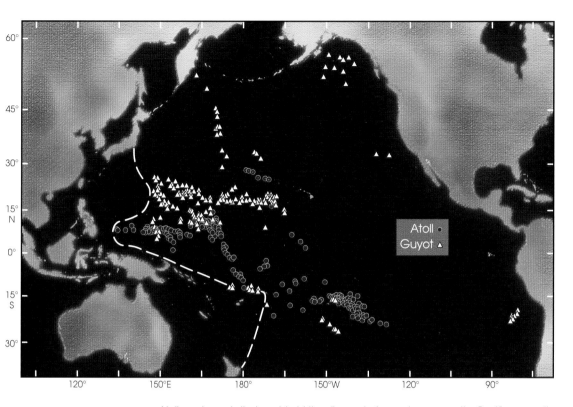

FIGURE 42. Atolls and guyots that could aid the dispersal of organisms across the Pacific are vastly more abundant to the south and west of Hawai'i than to the east.

When we look at corridors of dispersal in the north Pacific Ocean, what we find are dominant currents that originate in the far western Pacific near Taiwan and Japan and flow to the east toward Hawai'i. The strongest are the Subtropical Countercurrent (SCC) and the North Pacific Drift (NPD) (figure 43). Both spin off from the northward-flowing Kuroshio Current, forming two branches that turn east at latitudes of about 20 and 30 degrees respectively, north of the equator. The SCC often flows east at speeds up to 1 knot, and it passes through numerous island groups (southern Bonin Islands and Northern Marianas) and many solitary way stations like Wake and Johnston Atolls and over many intervening seamounts. The only current system to the east of Hawai'i is the Pacific North Equatorial Current (PNEC) that originates off California, and it tends to be rather weak (about 0.2 knots). During earlier times when the archipelago was in its infancy, these same basic current systems are thought to have existed but were much weaker. Thus in the ocean, the direction and the routes or pathways of dispersal of marine life to Hawai'i have been more or less the same since the origin of the archipelago seventy million–plus years ago. Even so, the fossil coral record reminds us that currents from the IWP may have been too weak to populate the islands for the first thirty-five million years, but after that, all the fossils from the southern Emperors and all the fossils in the Midway core are IWP in origin. In the modern day, 100 percent of the reef-building corals that exist in Hawai'i have their origins in the IWP.

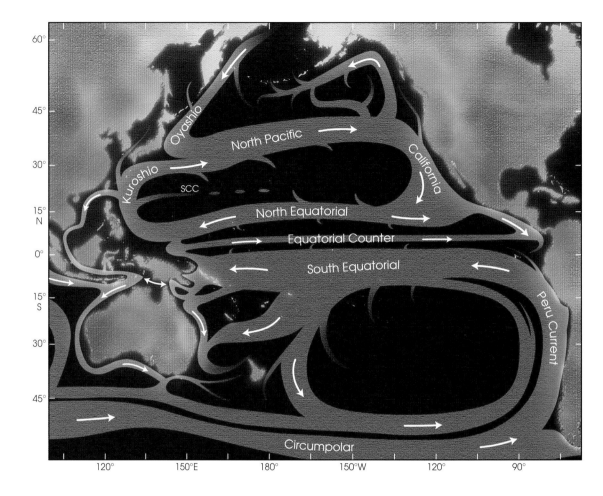

For colonization of the land, ocean currents may be sources of dispersal for some organisms, but we must also look at the winds and the flight patterns of birds. From the northwest and west, we find the upper-level Pacific jet stream and the north Pacific storms that usually travel west to east. From the east, there are the lower and more tropical trade winds that blow to the west. Both are sources for wind drifters and fliers. Insects, spiders, and crickets are good examples. Birds of course come from all directions, and they often carry with them spores, seeds, and even tangles of small animals such as insects and small land snails. Given all the possibilities of colonization from many directions to Hawai'i, it is perhaps surprising that our biota both in the ocean and the land is dominated by affinities to the IWP. Overall, 85 to 90 percent of Hawai'i's native biota is of Pacific origin compared to only 10 to 15 percent from North America. Even 90 percent of Hawai'i's insects, which are excellent fliers and therefore masters of dispersal, are thought to be of Pacific origin. The silverswords, fruit flies, and honeycreepers discussed earlier in this chapter are all species groups from the Americas, but in terms of colonization, they represent a minority source area. The overall picture tells us that the Hawaiian Archipelago is clearly more geographically isolated from the Americas than it is from the Pacific.

FIGURE 43. Major currents that transport larvae and flotsam to the Hawaiian Islands are SCC, NPD, and PNEC.

Attenuation across the Pacific

While native life in Hawai'i is extraordinarily beautiful and unique in evolutionary terms, we have learned that its overall diversity is very low due to its geographic isolation. Because life in Hawai'i is primarily IWP in origin, one way to measure its low diversity is to take stock of what is missing. The list is surprisingly long, but a few of the more dramatic examples might be mentioned. Before human contact, on land there were no coconut trees, bamboo, sugar cane, pineapples, amphibians, or reptiles, and there were only three mammals. In the ocean, there were no giant clams, fire corals, nautilus, abalone, or fiddler crabs, and there was only one species of grouper and one shallow-water sea fan. Another and even better way to document Hawai'i's loss in diversity is to plot the decline in genera or species of various biotic groups all the way across the Pacific (figure 44). For example, out of more than seven hundred species of coral that live in the IWP, only fifty-seven have made it to Hawai'i. Only those with the most long-lived larvae have survived the journey. The same pattern is true for a number of other invertebrates such as species of cowry shells. Not counting introduced species (discussed in chapter 6), only 10 percent of the IWP bird families are found to live naturally in Hawai'i. Only 15 percent of the IWP insects exist naturally in Hawai'i. Causal factors of attenuation include isolation due to distance, lack of stepping stones, the speeds and direction of intervening currents, longevity limits of marine larvae, spores and seeds, and limited flight or flightlessness in birds, and even limits in the habitats and general environmental conditions that exist in Hawai'i. Some organisms that reach Hawai'i cannot survive for one reason or another. One example is a species of poisonous sea snake that has been found alive in Hawai'i but fortunately it does not thrive or reproduce.

FIGURE 44. Attenuation of coral reef genera from west to east across the Pacific Ocean.

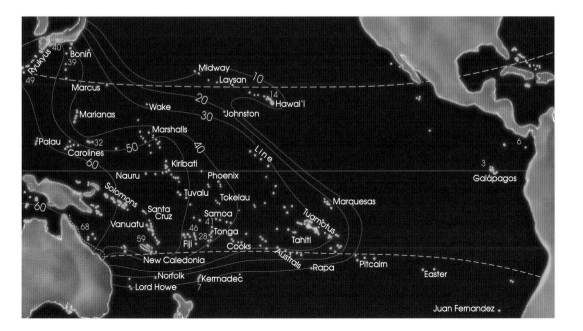

Differences between the Main Hawaiian Islands and the Northwestern Hawaiian Islands

On land, the differences between the Main Hawaiian Islands and the Northwestern Hawaiian Islands are huge, primarily a result of the drastically fewer habitats that are found on the latter. Except for two rocky islets (Nihoa and Necker; see figure 31, page 49) and two tiny pinnacles at French Frigate Shoals (see figure 32, page 49) and Gardner Pinnacles, terrestrial ecosystems in the NWHI, or Leeward Islands, are limited to low coastal and shoreline environments (see figure 33, page 49) and one small hypersaline lake on Laysan Island (see figure 38, page 59). As a result, only about 5 percent of the flora and fauna known from the Main Hawaiian Islands exists on various Leeward Islands. Nevertheless, several extremely unique species can be found there. Examples include trapdoor spiders and the vagrant grasshopper on Nihoa and several endemic birds on Nihoa and Laysan. Chapter 6 discusses human impact in greater detail, but other than the serious disturbances caused by guano miners and foreigners near the turn of the twentieth century, terrestrial ecosystems in the NWHI today are relatively pristine.

In contrast to the land, the differences in species composition between the MHI and the NWHI in the sea are much less significant, even though some of their habitats are quite different. The MHI have no atoll lagoons, while the NWHI have no brackish-water deep bays or shallow-water estuaries. Differences in species composition are the exception rather than the rule. Exotic examples are several species of reef fish (*Genicanthus* and sling-jaw wrasses) that exist exclusively in the NWHI.

The one great difference that does exist between the MHI and the NWHI in the marine realm is the vastly greater abundance of reef and shore fauna—reef fish, green sea turtles (figure 45), monk seals (figure 47), and marine birds (figures 46 and 48)—that reside in the NWHI. Nearly fourteen million Pacific seabirds are estimated to use the Leeward Islands as nesting grounds. Reflecting their pristine condition and lack of fishing pressure, the NWHI shallow-water ecosystems are dominated by top predators (sharks and ulua; figures 49 and 50). The biomass, or weight, of reef fishes overall in the NWHI has been estimated to be up to ten times greater than it is in the MHI (figure 51). More than 10 percent of the people in the MHI today are at least part-time fishermen! Management issues related to these differences are discussed in greater detail in chapter 6.

LEFT
FIGURE 45. The Hawaiian green sea turtle has increased in abundance about 500 percent since 1976, when it was listed as a threatened species.

BELOW
FIGURE 46.
An adult frigate bird (ʻiwa) about to take flight at French Frigate Shoals perhaps to go out fishing for breakfast.

ABOVE
FIGURE 47.
Hawaiian monk seals reside primarily in the Leeward Islands; in recent years, however, they have become more abundant in the Main Hawaiian Islands.

RIGHT
FIGURE 48.
On Midway Islands, a Laysan albatross feeds her chick by regurgitating food collected at sea.

ABOVE
FIGURE 49.
Galápagos sharks are among the fiercest top carnivores in the North-western Hawaiian Islands, and they are very abundant.

RIGHT
FIGURE 50.
The abundance of reef fish in the NWHI is up to ten times greater than in the MHI, primarily a result of over-fishing in the MHI.

NORTHWESTERN HAWAIIAN ISLANDS

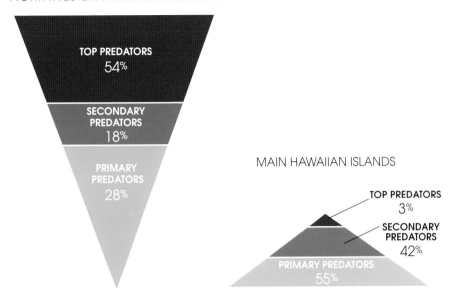

FIGURE 51. Fish biomass pyramids for the NWHI and the MHI. Note the opposite trophic (feeding) structure of apex predators, secondary predators, and primary predators in the two zones.

Life in the Deep Sea around Hawai'i

In earlier chapters, our voyage touched down several times in the deep sea around the Hawaiian Islands and seamounts, first on a maiden dive to Lō'ihi and again in the Milwaukee Seamounts where huge beds of precious coral and fossil reef corals millions of years old exist. Remarkably, we find many of the same live communities of deep-sea organisms from Lō'ihi all the way to the Emperor Seamounts in similar depth zones where differences in temperature and salinity are small. Lō'ihi Seamount and the Milwaukee Seamounts are separated by over two thousand miles of ocean, not to mention all the gaps between the intervening volcanic edifices.

During the 1970s and '80s, I was chief scientist aboard sixteen exploratory oceanographic expeditions to investigate the deep precious coral fauna of Hawai'i. Our cruises spanned the chain at mid depths from Hawai'i to Midway Islands and slightly beyond to Hancock Seamount. During these series of cruises, collectively known as the Sango Expedition, we conducted 183 dredge hauls, using tangle net dredges, and made ten submersible dives in the two-man *Star II* submersible. Overall, we discovered six commercial-size beds of precious coral, three in the NWHI and three in the MHI. The MHI beds serve as the source of precious red, pink, and gold corals that are presently used in the precious coral industry in Hawai'i (figure 52). Today all the beds in the NWHI are protected in perpetuity under provisions in President George W. Bush's Executive Order in 2006 that redefined the NWHI as a marine national monument.

The biological similarity that exists in all the precious coral beds across thousands of miles of submerged volcanic island shelves or seamounts suggests uniformity in physical and chemical conditions in the overlying waters at these depths. The extreme patchiness of the coral beds turns out to be a result of similar patchiness in habitat requirements, which include a bottom substrata that is clean-swept and firm, either limestone or lava, and very strong bottom currents.

In contrast to the uniformity of physical and chemical conditions at midwater depths across the island archipelago, coral reefs at or near the surface are exposed to very large differences in temperature and sunlight across the chain, and as we saw in chapter 4, Hawai'i's coral islands eventually drown at the Darwin Point where temperature and light are too low to support the upward growth of corals.

In the deep sea, precious coral beds continue to thrive for almost one thousand miles more to the north of the Darwin Point. In the 1970s and '80s, Japanese and Taiwanese coral fishermen dredged more than several hundred tons of pink coral from the shelves of the remote Emperor Seamounts and Guyots. Unfortunately these ancient Hawaiian volcanoes exist outside the United States' two-hundred-mile Exclusive Economic Zone and the United States was, and still is, unable to restrict or manage the foreign fleets. Today most of the Emperor Seamounts' precious coral beds are thought to be depleted, although future surveys are needed to document their condition.

FIGURE 52. A colony of precious red coral photographed from the port of the *Pisces 5* submersible at a depth of sixteen hundred feet off South Point on the Big Island of Hawai'i.

CORAL REEFS IN HAWAI'I TODAY
HEALTHIER THAN YOU THINK

This morning, I am looking out of my living room window at the ocean off east O'ahu, just ten miles from Honolulu. It is mid-January 2011, in the middle of winter; it is also the middle of the rainy season, and huge waves are pounding the north shores of all the Hawaiian Islands. Yesterday, the coastal ocean water was chocolate brown virtually everywhere on O'ahu and probably many of the other Main Hawaiian Islands. Surfers were warned to stay out of the water since the runoff into the ocean contained an abundance of waterborne bacteria and other disease-causing organisms. Almost anyone looking at the dirty brown ocean might think the coral reefs must be dying under such a cloud of mud and silt. And so the question arises: How healthy are Hawai'i's coral reefs?

By now readers know that I am a coral reef ecologist at the University of Hawai'i, where I have been conducting research for almost forty years. Over this time, I have been extremely fortunate to have visited every island in the Hawaiian Chain that stretches across fourteen hundred miles of the north Pacific from the Big Island of Hawai'i in the southeast to Midway Islands and Kure Atoll in the northwest. Together with colleagues and students, I have studied coral reefs in their every habitat and niche, from the shallow reef flats to the deepest twilight zones where even black and pink precious corals are found. In the early 1970s our team measured the growth of corals on a series of dated underwater lava flows on the Big Island of Hawai'i that go back to 1801. What we discovered is that a mature coral reef in Hawai'i takes about fifty years or more to fully develop. Considering their thickness, of course, most reefs are much older than this, and if we include fossil reef structures, some reef deposits are as old as the islands themselves, going back millions of years. During the 1980s, our team also measured the growth of coral on reefs all the way up the island chain to the very end at Kure Atoll. What we found among other things already discussed (see chapter 4) was that the reefs were healthy everywhere, except their growth rate gradually declined the farther north they grew as the water temperature cooled and the day length shortened. We also discovered that the major factor controlling the abundance of reef corals was very large but episodic wave events, not dissimilar from forest fires in many places on the land.

Muddy water and healthy coral reefs present an interesting paradox. How can coral reefs in Hawai'i be so healthy if they are sometimes covered by sediment-laden brown water carried into the ocean from land runoff? The answer to this question requires that we first distinguish between reefs near the shore inside the breaker zone and those coral reefs that lie outside the surf in deeper water. We must also distinguish between reefs exposed to large quantities of fresh-water runoff from the land versus those reefs where runoff is minimal or non-existent. In other words, there are many different kinds of habitats in Hawai'i where corals exist. Perhaps the easiest way to explain the paradox is to compare the best habitats to the worst habitats. The reefs that I have described above on lava flows or off the islands in the extended Hawaiian Chain all exist outside the breaker zone at depths of thirty to one hundred feet, and all are in well-mixed and relatively clear water. These zones are generally considered optimal, although some very robust reefs can be found shallower or deeper.

Next let's talk about the worst zones. Typically these areas are found inside the surf zone, such as shallow reef flats, or in bays or in otherwise confined or enclosed areas (Pearl Harbor, etc.). Water circulation in such areas is often very poor, and as a result, when large amounts of water runoff enter the ocean, it is not readily mixed or transported offshore. Instead, these zones are like incubation pools. Suspended sediments may settle out on the bottom and suffocate marine life. The lack of mixing may give way to brackish-water conditions with low salinity and high nutrient concentrations (phosphate, nitrate, and silicate). These conditions are often quite favorable for algae rather than corals, and indeed, the reefs in such zones are more often dominated by various species of algae. Corals may be rare or even nonexistent depending on the degree of mixing and circulation. Chocolate-brown water entering such habitats may linger for days or even weeks depending on the frequency of heavy rains or mixing induced by strong winds or wave-generated currents. Efforts to save these types of "reefs" from land runoff and pollution may be ill-considered since they normally do not support healthy coral reefs. Attempts to remove alien algae from such habitats may be equally frustrating since the algae will most likely just grow back.

This does not mean that we should not try to generally improve land management and reduce the runoff of brown water into the ocean. There are many examples where it could make a huge difference. Off the south coast of Moloka'i, there is excessive runoff of sediment-laden water due to the trampling of upland areas by invasive and wild populations of hoofed mammals such as goats, axis deer, and sheep. Many of these species were introduced by the state into unfenced land to provide a resource for hunting interests. Unfortunately, the state policy regarding these animals is to release and forget them. This policy void could easily be corrected by fencing restrictions and population control. Lacking such action, the reef flats along about thirty miles of the southeastern coast are frequently inundated by sediment-laden runoff that originates in highly eroded uplands, home to the feral ungulates.

Another example is the whole island of Kaho'olawe, which used to be a bomb site for the US Navy. During this time, sediment runoff caused by bombing and rainfall laid waste to coral reefs around the entire island. When the bombing stopped in 1990, it took two decades for the reefs to recover. But the good news is that they did recover, once the source of sediment runoff had been eliminated.

The south end of Kāne'ohe Bay is yet another example where proper management has led to a major recovery of the coral reefs in the bay. Prior to 1976, a sewer outfall discharged sewage directly into the south bay. The reefs living there were virtually destroyed. But in 1976 the outfall was removed from the bay and relocated offshore into the open ocean at a depth of 110 feet, and the sewage was treated at the secondary level. The reefs in the bay responded immediately by beginning a slow but steady long-term recovery, and the coral reefs outside the bay were unaffected by the new outfall.

There are many other small habitats on reef flats or in bays in Hawai'i that could be improved by better watershed management. Land areas laid bare by the harvest of large tracts of pineapple or other crops, or by land development, need to be immediately replanted. Upland areas need to be reforested. Feral pigs and ungulates need to be controlled. The land needs to be viewed as a garden and treated accordingly.

Looking again at the offshore reefs in Hawai'i, the main reason why many if not most of these reefs are healthy is because they are beyond the negative influences of the land. This is especially true in the Northwestern Hawaiian Islands where there is virtually no runoff from the land. The islands there are simply too small or too low to generate significant runoff.

Now that we have distinguished the differences between the inshore and offshore reefs in Hawai'i, there is yet another aspect to the paradox of reef health in Hawai'i, and this involves overfishing. Hawai'i's offshore coral reefs in the high islands, especially O'ahu, are extremely overfished. Decreases in the abundance of reef fish range between 70 to 90 percent of levels that existed one hundred years ago. Today about 10 percent of the human population in the Hawaiian Islands are fishermen of one sort or another. Unfortunately, the state is almost invisible when it comes to enforcement. I have been a recreational fishermen for more than forty years in Hawai'i, and I have never seen a fish and game warden. Of course they exist, but unfortunately they spend most of their time eradicating marijuana in the upland forests. The solution to the problem is more wardens but also a much stronger conservation ethic. The state could also convert more of the coastline to "conservation districts." Less than 1 percent of the coastline in the state is protected from fishing today. The state could also build more artificial reefs.

How most coral reefs in Hawai'i stay so healthy without normal levels of reef fish is another intriguing question. There are fifty-seven species of reef-building corals in Hawai'i, and interestingly very few, if any, actually depend on the reef fish for their survival. Of course, many symbiotic relations between the corals and the fish exist but not at a level of survivorship for the corals. But, I should hasten to add, the other way around is not true; many species of reef fish do depend on live corals for their survival.

In summary, the paradox of healthy versus dying coral reefs in Hawai'i has many sources. Many kinds of coral reefs exist and need to be distinguished. One size does not fit all. Inshore reef ecosystems are generally dominated by algae; in fact they could be called coral-algal associations. Offshore reefs are predominately healthy, although most are seriously overfished, particularly in the major high islands. It is commonplace to hear that coral reefs in Hawai'i are polluted or even in crisis. The source of this misunderstanding is often the press, where attention usually focuses on worst-case scenarios. Bad news sells, or you could say, "Why talk about nonproblems?" Also when it comes to coral reefs, a long view is necessary. Coral reefs require many decades to develop, and therefore snapshots of conditions over the short term more often distort than clarify the true picture. Finally, coral reefs are very hardy, even resilient, in spite of chocolate-brown water or too many fishermen. What sometimes looks very bad might only be the ephemeral aftermath of a bad storm. In fact, as I look out of my living room window this afternoon, the water is already starting to clear up. Every cloud has a silver lining.

SUMMARY

In summary, life in Hawai'i can be said to be a very special "Garden of Eden" (figure 53), but comparatively speaking, the islands are inhabited by a very exclusive membership. The Hawaiian Archipelago is the oldest chain of islands in the world. Even so, its flora and fauna on the land and in the sea is extremely young relative to the age of the islands, and cycles of extinction and recolonization are common in both biospheres. The maximum evolutionary age of the majority of species in the sea and on land in the Hawaiian Islands is generally less than five million years, whereas the age of the islands range up to thirty million and the seamounts and guyots up to seventy million–plus years.

Overall, the biota of the land and the sea in Hawai'i is characterized by very low diversity due primarily to isolation of the archipelago on both land and under the sea from source areas. But there are also major differences between land and marine ecosystems. On land, the flora and fauna is very specialized and contains many examples of species groups that have undergone spectacular adaptive radiation with many species per genus. In contrast, the marine biota is much more generalized and is characterized by few species per genus. Habitat diversity on land is much greater than it is in the sea, and at least twice as many species live on the land than in the sea. Clearly, rates of evolution and speciation in Hawai'i are much faster on land than in the sea.

Comparatively, the land is even more isolated than the sea from sources of colonization. At the species level, in the modern time, colonization down the chain, especially on land, appears to be limited primarily to the large high Hawaiian Islands from Ni'ihau to the Big Island. Nevertheless, the main source area for the vast majority (80 to 90 percent) of the flora and fauna of all the Hawaiian Islands is the "greater" Pacific, via the IWP center of origin.

Interestingly, the first humans to discover Hawai'i were Polynesians, who, as we shall see, followed similar routes from the IWP, via many similar island stepping stones, and ultimately they took pathways that led them to the same destination as the many, many species of both plants and animals that preceded them.

FIGURE 53. Lush rain forests can be found on all the high Hawaiian Islands on windward coastlines at mid elevations most commonly in deep valleys.

CHAPTER 6

HUMAN CONTACT

POLYNESIANS DISCOVER HAWAI'I

Thus far our voyage to the Hawaiian Archipelago has only considered natural processes and events. The first five chapters cover the geological origin and fate of Hawai'i's islands and seamounts as well as the history of their flora and fauna. The final chapter must logistically be the one written by human contact: first by the Polynesians and then, more than a thousand years later, by the European explorers, and all who followed. The full story of human history in Hawai'i has been told and retold in numerous other volumes and places, and while it is briefly summarized here, the main purpose of this chapter is to investigate the impact of human contact both on the life and on the land.

Discovery of Hawai'i by the Polynesians is often described as one of the greatest navigational feats in human history. Retracing the questions of why, when, and how pulls together humankind's basic instincts of wanderlust, restlessness, and courage. Perhaps the best place to pick up the historical thread would be the time when prehistoric voyagers wandered east out of Southeast Asia in search of new islands in the vast Pacific.

About thirty-five hundred years ago, the peoples of Southeast Asia's islands began an eastward migration. As islanders, they were canoe-building people who had learned to carve wood into huge hulls and create sails out of woven pandanus leaves and tie them together with yards and yards of sennit. The Austronesians, as they are sometimes called, in reference to their common lan-guages, ventured eastward out of Taiwan, the Philippines, and Indonesia, into the Bismark Archipelago and into the Solomon Islands, New Hebrides, and New Caledonia, eventually landing in Fiji around 3300 BP (before present). They carried with them pigs, dogs, and chickens and a multitude of plants

FIGURE 54. Artistic rendition depicting Polynesian landfall in Hawai'i.

and, of course, food stores and water to survive voyages of unknown distance and time. These were not accidental trips, nor were they the result of happenstance drift. They were purposeful acts of discovery, and they had to be carefully planned and executed. But this is not to say that all were successful.

The question of "why" has been pondered over and over and probably has many answers. Perhaps the first thing to consider is that these were trips between islands, and life on an island has unique attributes. Obviously, overpopulation can occur faster in a smaller place. Islands are sometimes quite vulnerable to natural disasters that could trigger evacuation, temporary or permanent. Primogeniture, the custom of some native cultures of leaving the majority of the family wealth (land, home, animals, crops) to the oldest son, may have caused younger sons to migrate. There may also have been an ancestral memory in the populations of many Southeast Asians of there always being more islands to the east. The swath of ocean that lies across the southwestern Pacific is literally strewn with islands that stretch eastward from Asia for more than five thousand miles. Faith in sailing farther east would not have been blind. Trips could also be planned to head back to the west at some middle point when half of the stores were gone.

While this book is about the Hawaiian Archipelago, the history of human colonization across the Pacific may contain many ecological lessons that might logically replay in the Hawaiian Islands. It is thus interesting to reexamine the great Polynesian diaspora. Once the Austronesians reached the island of Fiji, they seemed to remain settled for a longer period of time during which they developed a unique culture. Known as the Lapita cultural complex, it is often identified with beautiful cooking pottery that was of unusual high quality and fabrication (figure 55). This culture appeared to link together societies in the Melanesian island arcs across to the Fiji-Samoa-Tonga triangle. Archeological evidence suggests that this population complex persisted for about one thousand years before further dispersal to the east occurred. Fiji in particular is a relatively large and mountainous group of islands that might well have supported very large populations. For some reason, toward the end of the Lapita cultural dominance, their distinctive ceramic craftsmanship seemed to diminish, replaced by more crudely fashioned Polynesian ware and later on by products made of wood. There seemed to be a transfer from the use of broad-based soil, clay, and rock materials to more frequent use of volcanic rocks and woods. A more elaborate and sophisticated technology for fishing and marine exploitation also began to emerge. About the time of Christ and for the next few centuries, the Polynesians would continue to push east along an environmental gradient or trend toward smaller islands and reduced habitat diversity. The landscape in Fiji is of continental origin, whereas all the islands to the east are oceanic, derived entirely by volcanic activity. Both habitats, however, are surrounded by coral reefs, possibly explaining the increased reliance on fishing technologies.

Sometime over the next five hundred years, or at least by 800 AD, the final phase of Polynesian discovery went forward, first east through the Society Islands and Tahiti and then to the Marquesas, and from there to the far-flung corners of the Polynesian triangle, Hawaiʻi, Easter Island and back to New Zealand (figure 56). In Hawaiʻi, a second wave of migration is thought to have taken place between about 1100 and 1300 AD consisting primarily of double-hulled canoes from Tahiti. During this time, two-way contact between Tahiti and Hawaiʻi may have been established. The significance or even frequency of long-distance voyaging between Tahiti and Hawaiʻi is suggested by the ancient name of the channel leading south from Maui between Lānaʻi and Kahoʻolawe. It is called the Kealaikahiki Channel, and because k's in Hawaiian are t's in Tahitian, the name of the channel means "pathway to Tahiti."

That travel between Tahiti and Hawaiʻi could have been a frequent occurrence refocuses attention on the whole question of Polynesian navigational skill. Interestingly, one of the first people to raise this question was one of the greatest ocean navigators who ever lived, Captain James Cook, the famous European explorer who charted the Hawaiian Islands in 1778 and 1779. Cook is said to have exclaimed, "How could a stone-age people have navigated and explored a third of the Earth's surface without instruments and charts? How could they have built powerful sailing vessels without metal nails or canvas sails?" Cook's doubts about Polynesian navigational skills have been raised by

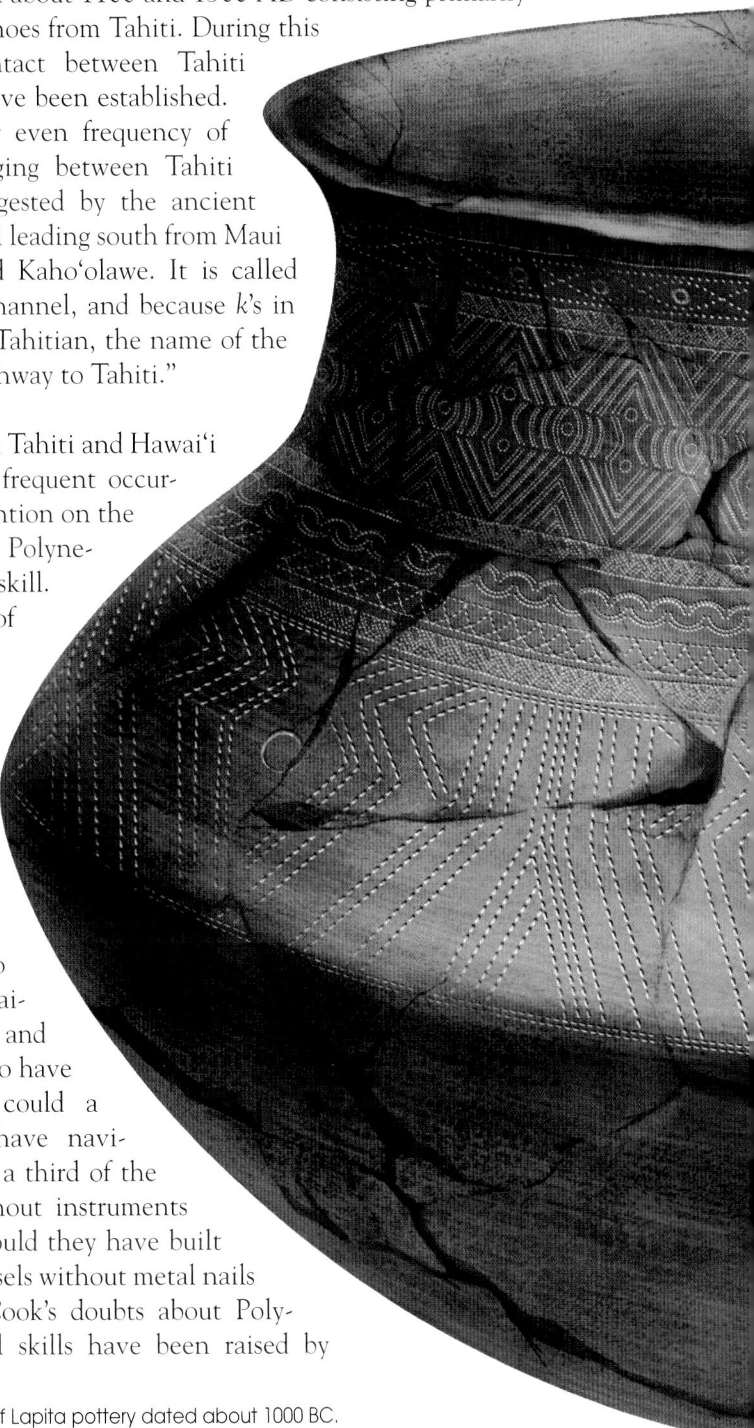

FIGURE 55. An illustration of Lapita pottery dated about 1000 BC.

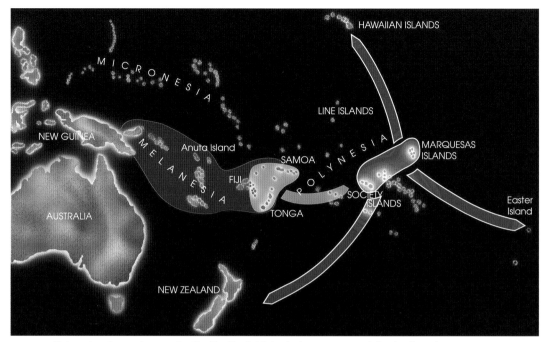

FIGURE 56. Polynesian dispersal across the Pacific. The light shaded area represents the Lapita culture in Fiji, whereas the directional arrows illustrate probable routes of long-distance voyaging.

numerous other sources both skeptical and supportive. Was their navigation accidental or purposeful? Was discovery purely by chance, perhaps by fishing canoes that had been blown out to sea or somehow lost? And again, what forces could have been strong enough to motivate such extraordinary long-distance travel? Some scholars have even suggested that South American Indians could have settled Polynesia, by simply drifting westward in prevailing winds and currents. Presence of the South American sweet potato in Polynesia gives some credence to this theory, as does Thor Heyerdahl's famous crossing of the east Pacific from Peru to the Tuamotu Islands in 1947 in the raft *Kon-Tiki*.

It was this atmosphere of question and doubt that led to another experiment that would inspire the building of a double-hulled canoe designed to replicate those of the ancient Marquesans and Tahitians. The canoe would test the theory that Hawai'i was intentionally discovered by highly skilled Polynesian navigators. It would therefore be necessary to recruit a master navigator from somewhere in the Pacific Islands. The project was a vision of the Polynesian Voyaging Society (PVS) founded in 1973 by Dr. Ben Finney, an anthropologist at the University of Hawai'i; Herb Kane, a Hawaiian artist; and Tommy Holmes, a writer and waterman. The voyaging canoe would be named *Hōkūle'a*, the Hawaiian name for the star Arcturus, Hawai'i's zenith star.

On May 1, 1976, *Hōkūle'a* left Hawai'i under sail for Tahiti and under the leadership of Mau Piailug, one of the last known master navigators in the Pacific Islands. Thirty-three days later, thousands of Tahitians would welcome Mau and his entourage of Hawaiians, many of whom were actually ancestors of ancient Tahitians. It was a momentous event of pride and joy, as if a long-lost family had finally been reunited. *Hōkūleʻa* would become a symbol of cultural revival. The voyage had renewed a long-forgotten spirit. It would be recognition that the greatest navigational instrument of all was the navigator himself. It was validation that his values were the same as those of all the seafarers who had preceded him for more than three thousand years.

The navigator would have to put to memory the relative location of rising and setting stars, the sun, as well as the direction of easterly trade winds and when these winds might switch and blow from the west. The navigator would understand and memorize the flight patterns of migratory birds such as the Pacific golden plover and shore birds like terns and noddys, whose flight patterns reverse from daybreak to dusk. At first light, they fly out to sea to fish and then return to their island roosts at day's end. The navigator could also recognize swell directions and interference patterns that would reveal the presence of upstream islands. The navigator would also know that large islands attract high cumulus clouds and that the green reflection on the undersides of lower clouds were reflections from atoll lagoons. The navigator would know that atolls could only be seen from a distance of five to ten miles, large islands less than one hundred miles. The navigator would be deeply tuned to the natural elements surrounding his voyage. Once a new island had been discovered, the navigator and his people would take his knowledge and way of being ashore, and it would shape the course of their settlement for at least those years before something stirred and renewed their migration.

In the case of the *Hōkūleʻa*'s maiden voyage from Hawaiʻi to Tahiti, after the celebrations of arrival in Tahiti had ended, Mau Piailug left the ship to Kawika Kapehulehua, who would captain the canoe back to Hawaiʻi. Nainoa Thompson would later spend several years training and learning all that he could from Mau, and for the next three decades, he would lead six more voyages across the Pacific to all corners of the ocean. Once again it would take vision, planning, discipline, courage, and even sacrifice. The voyages of *Hōkūleʻa* would mark a renaissance of cultural revival that would encompass the entire Pacific. In Hawaiʻi, it would commemorate Polynesian discovery and recognize their original values. As we explore the centuries after first landfall up through Western contact, the values that served the ancient Polynesians may also be values that need to be relearned by modern society today.

LANDFALL

Nainoa Thompson has described "finding landfall as a test of perseverance," but he humbly omits to say that there are no guarantees. The Polynesians in the first canoe (or canoes) to land in Hawaiʻi must have been elated beyond anything we can imagine today (figure 54). I was once lost at sea during a sail from Hawaiʻi to Tahiti in 1959. It was somewhere near the equator hundreds of miles from any island. It would only be an hour before the vessel on which I had been sailing turned around and returned to pick me up, but it was long enough for me to rethink my entire life up until that point. Another personal brush with being lost at sea was in 1978, when on its second trip to Tahiti, the *Hōkūleʻa* foundered in the Molokaʻi Channel, and Eddie Aikau was lost at sea. As part of the rescue effort, I had taken the University of Hawaiʻi ship *Holokai* into the Molokaʻi Channel for eight hours the next day in search of Eddie. The wind was blowing forty-five knots and gusting to sixty. The seas were twenty feet high or higher and were breaking everywhere. The ocean surface was covered with foam. The air was filled with spray. We didn't find Eddie, but we may have shared in his final thoughts. I am sure that some of the original canoes that left the Marquesas about twelve hundred years ago in search of land to the north never found it, in spite of all their navigational skills. It is with this respect that I begin the story of the first Polynesians to make landfall and colonize Hawaiʻi.

Little is known about first landfall in Hawaiʻi other than what can be inferred from archeological traces. The earliest sites that have been excavated on the Big Island of Hawaiʻi suggest that the first canoes to land were from the Marquesas Islands around 800 AD plus or minus one hundred years. Artifacts including adzes, fishhooks (figure 57), and pendants are all of Marquesan design of pearl, shell, and bone. The Marquesas Islands are also closest to Hawaiʻi, and their eastern longitude marks them as the best point of departure to locate islands to the far north and west. Trade winds in both hemispheres are from the east, and therefore canoes traveling north would tend to track downwind to the west. The Marquesans would probably have had the navigational skills of a Mau Piailug, but initially they would not have known what star to follow or what course to steer. A successful course would require travel about 30 degrees of latitude to the north, about eighteen hundred nautical miles, on a bearing about 30 degrees west of north. They may well have followed the North Star, Polaris, which is stationary in the night sky, and the trade winds would have carried them 15 to 20 degrees of longitude downwind, just westerly enough to land somewhere in the high islands of Hawaiʻi. Once within the high islands, navigation between them could be done by sight alone.

It is also probable that landfall was achieved by simultaneous arrival of more than one canoe since a propagule of less than perhaps one hundred people would have led to inbreeding and a decreased chance of survival. But not only did the Hawaiians survive, they did so quite successfully. Looking back at their history, their survival perhaps should be credited to at least thirty generations of ancestral experience in what might be called transportation technology: not only navigational skills but also the ability to transport a portable agricultural system that included a multitude of plants, seedlings, and cuttings, as well as pigs, dogs, and chickens. The Hawaiians had planned to become permanent residents in their new land.

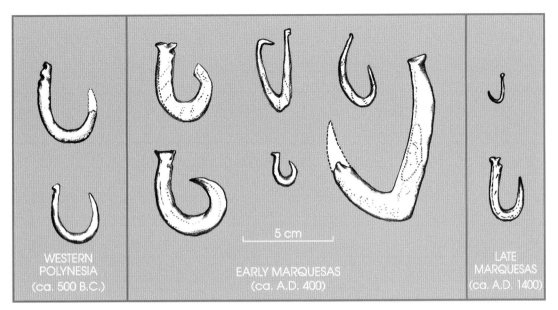

WESTERN
POLYNESIA
(ca. 500 B.C.)

EARLY MARQUESAS
(ca. A.D. 400)

5 cm

LATE
MARQUESAS
(ca. A.D. 1400)

FIGURE 57. Fishhooks of early Marquesan design have been found in early excavations in Hawai`i.

HAWAIIAN COLONIZATION AND IMPACT

While it is difficult if not impossible to detail the chronology of environmental impact of native colonization on the Hawaiian Islands, we do know that their arrival drastically transformed the landscape and the natural flora and fauna. Of the at least thirty new species the Polynesians brought with them, the most significant were coconuts; bamboo; sugar cane; breadfruit; ti; yam; bottle gourd; taro; rice grass; sweet potatoes; bananas; mountain apples; *kukui* trees; various larger domestic animals, mainly pigs, dogs, and chickens; and a number of unintended stowaways like skinks, geckos, and rats.

One of the first big changes that took place after landfall was the clearing of lowland forests to make way for living space and shelter. As populations grew, more and more land would need to be cleared. The method used was slashing and burning of lowland forest ecosystems. This would result in the extirpation of many lowland endemic and indigenous species. Perhaps one of the best indicators of ecological impact is the number and date of settlements and housing sites. These sites in turn can be used to infer population growth. The largest human impact on the environment was, of course, the impact of humans themselves. Archeological data collected by Patrick Kirch and others show that, initially, population growth was slow for several hundred years, but then between 1000 and 1200 AD, a developmental phase took place throughout the islands (figure 58), and the population began to rapidly climb.

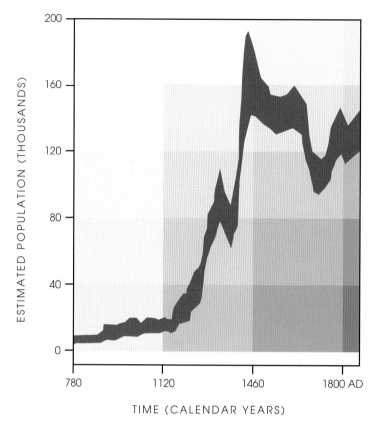

FIGURE 58. One estimation of the Hawaiian population throughout the islands based on wood-charcoal excavations. The brown area is an estimate of the margin of error of this study.

This phase was soon followed by a period of even more rapid expansion that lasted another four hundred years until about 1500 or 1700 AD. What the population number was at its peak is controversial, but both Kirch and the wood-charcoal data favor a maximum figure of about two hundred thousand people. This number contrasts sharply with an estimate of four hundred thousand given by Lieutenant James King on board Captain Cook's Resolution in 1779. Captain George Dixon on board another foreign vessel in 1787 projected that a population of two hundred thousand in 1779 would have actually been much closer to the truth. As important as the number is, the possibility that it represents a value close to the carrying capacity of the islands for a subsistence economy is even more significant. Also if a contraction in numbers did occur one hundred or two hundred years before Western contact, this would place the estimate of the maximum number of the Hawaiian population in peak years at about three hundred thousand.

With this estimate in hand, and knowing the Hawaiian population had spread to all the islands, the aggregate impact on the environment must have been very large. The transformation of the lowlands was particularly significant. Captain Cook and his officers had noted that in 1779, four or five miles of lowland areas on the Big Island had been cleared. The British explorer George Vancouver reported in the 1790s that the lower half of the island of Kaua'i had been deforested presumably by slash-and-burn cultivation, creating an open grassland of ferns and shrubs. Large valley bottoms like those at Hanalei on Kaua'i, Mākaha on O'ahu, Hālawa on Moloka'i, and Waimea on the Big Island were converted to pond-fields for taro farming. During the period of dramatic population increase around 1300–1400 AD, even upland slopes were terraced for agriculture such as those preserved above Lapakahi on the Big Island. The building of human settlements, *heiau*, lava rock walls, and other cultural structures further altered the landscape. Hunting and gathering expanded. Birds were captured for food, and their feathers were used to make splendid capes and cloaks for the Hawaiian *ali'i* (chiefs). During processions of the *ali'i*, large poles festooned with bird feathers called *kāhili* were commonplace in cultural celebrations. Before Western contact, more than one-third of Hawai'i's native avifauna was driven to extinction. More than one hundred species of land snails also disappeared, mostly due to habitat destruction.

Not all the changes brought about by the Hawaiians were negative. In fact, much of the land was managed in pie-shaped units called *ahupua'a* that extended from the mountains to the sea. A system of taboos, or *kapu*, was organized to control the exploitation of resources. Violation of the *kapu* often resulted in severe punishment, even death. A conservation ethic in Hawaiian culture was also evident by the Hawaiians constructing extensive fishponds. Fishponds were large holding pens built with lava rocks that extended out over many shallow reefs in order to encircle and hold many species of fish, especially mullet and milkfish (figure 59). It is also noteworthy that no marine resources are known to have been overexploited before Western contact.

FIGURE 59.
Typical Hawaiian fishpond on the south coast of O'ahu.

In spite of these harmonious traditions, increasing population growth led to greater competition for resources, impacting not only the flora and fauna but also the Hawaiians themselves. The rise of social stratification, chiefs, managers (*konohiki*), stricter *kapu*, and eventually warfare between island populations might be considered evidence of heightened competition for resources at or beyond carrying capacity. In today's vernacular, this ecological condition is sometimes called "the tragedy of the commons." Unfortunately, many island ecosystems that have been impacted by human colonization have fallen victim to this outcome. One of the best known examples is Rapa Nui, or Easter Island, where massive deforestation occurred to support human settlements and to transport their massive stone sculptures known as *aku-aku*, eventually leading to resource depletion, social disintegration, and warfare.

WESTERN CONTACT

Once again, it should be emphasized that the purpose here is not to rewrite the history of Western contact but rather to describe its overall impact on the land and its life. To do so requires that we again examine human population growth and those events and commercial developments that shaped the next two hundred years of Hawai'i's future. Humans of course play an integral role in the ecosystem at large that might be viewed as an enormous pyramid of energy, food, diversity, and production, in which impacts run from the bottom up as well as the top down. Those from the top down are generally driven by the top predators or top consumers, which in this case are human beings.

Although several other European explorers might have visited the Hawaiian Islands before the epic third voyage of Captain Cook in 1779, it was contact by his ship that figuratively began "Western contact" and opened the door to what would become a flood of migrants to the islands from virtually every direction in the world that continues to this day. Captain Cook had warned his crew to avoid sexual contact with the Hawaiians but that was like banning the trade winds or the falling rain. It was the beginning of what are sometimes called "virgin soil epidemics." At first it was mostly a trickle of venereal disease, but with the continued arrival of visitors in the following decades—whalers, sandalwood traders, missionaries, and many, many more—the trickle turned into a series of major epidemics such as influenza, small pox, measles, dysentery, and scarlet fever, all of which took a tremendous toll on native Hawaiians. Unfortunately, the Hawaiians had no natural immunity to almost all these diseases. In 1832, when the first census was carried out by the missionaries, the population of native Hawaiians was only 130,313 people. Recalling estimates of the Hawaiian population in 1779 that ranged between two hundred thousand to four hundred thousand, the overall decline may have been as much as 35 to 70 percent. Unfortunately, the decline had not ended there.

There was also baggage in the flood of incoming migrants. It was a myriad of alien species, many of which had a major negative impact on the environment as well as humans. Besides missionaries, whalers, and traders, their galleons brought mosquitoes, cockroaches, termites, ants, fleas, wasps, and many other uninvited guests to Hawai'i. It was an inauspicious beginning of a new wave of introduced species rearranging Hawai'i's ecosystems, some by filling empty niches, others by competing for space or food, and still others by causing more extinction of the native flora and fauna. As we have seen, the native biota had already suffered dozens of introductions from Polynesia; however, the pace of change was beginning to dramatically quicken.

Before discussing the cumulative changes brought about by Western contact in more detail, it might be insightful to pause and look at some of the major waves of social change that would facilitate the process. Two of the most important transitions were the breakdown of *kapu* and gradual changes in land tenure. The death of King Kamehameha in 1819 coincided with the upsurge in the breaking of *kapu*, especially by Hawaiian women. The next king of Hawai'i, Liholiho, the son of King Kamehameha, would in fact abolish the *kapu* altogether. In the following year, 1820, missionaries from New England began to arrive, and their mission of introducing Christianity into Hawaiian culture began filling the void. In spite of good intentions and partial success to convert the Hawaiians and shift their world, their influence overall had little effect on conserving the environment. Unfortunately, preaching truths that every good Christian could agree with did not replace the *kapu* in terms of protecting the environment. If anything, Christianity contributed to the disintegration of native customs and dismantled traditional land tenure.

One of the worst impacts associated with missionary influence was their effort to help the ruling chiefs organize their government. In 1840 the first constitution was written. Soon after, the government began to reapportion the land beginning with what is known as the Great *Mahele*. By 1850, the notion of private property was introduced, and for the first time, foreigners were allowed to purchase large tracts of land. Production of sugar cane had started in 1835, and the Great *Mahele* gave impetus to investment in the land, including large plots that could be used for agriculture. Sugar production would greatly benefit the Hawaiian economy, but it would also transform huge tracts of land as native ecosystems were replaced with sugar cane. It would also require the diversion of water and would consume vast quantities of wood to process the cane into molasses and sugar. Finally, increasing sugar production would create a great need for labor, and since the Hawaiian population continued to decline, contract labor was recruited actively from overseas countries, mainly from China, Japan, Korea, the Philippines, and Portugal. This would contribute to an enormous increase in the resident population.

Jumping ahead to the next century, pineapple production began around 1900, and it too would commit a great number of acres to agricultural development. Other major events or trends in the twentieth century that would significantly increase human population were World War II and tourism (figure 60).

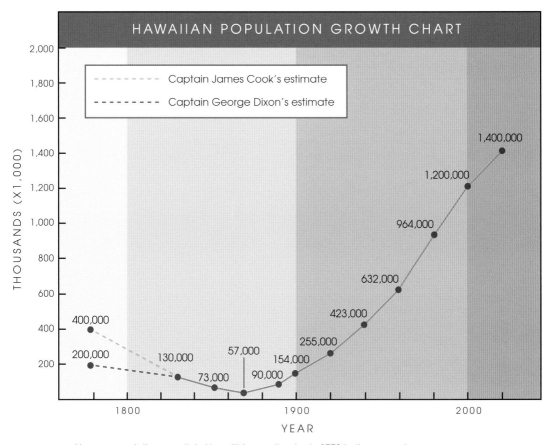

FIGURE 60. Human population growth in Hawai'i from estimates in 1779 to the present.

Between 1800 and 1900, the population first fell to a low of 57,000 in 1872, but then it doubled in the next thirty years. Since 1900 it has doubled again three times over, rising from 154,000 to more than 1.4 million today. Although this review of population growth in Hawai'i is extraordinarily brief, its significance regarding environmental impact is of enormous importance. Human impact over the past two hundred years has truly transformed the land and the life in Hawai'i. Today, virtually every lowland landscape is so dominated by alien species that it would be unrecognizable to the first human arrivals from Polynesia. While not discounting Polynesian impacts, especially the carnage to the land flora caused by their pigs and the extinction of the avifauna due to their dogs, the ecological footprint caused by Western contact has been several orders of magnitude greater. Looking at just the numbers of introductions and extinctions of endemic and indigenous species, we can begin to recognize the differences before and after 1779.

As for introductions, plants provide the best example. Compared to about thirty species brought in by the Polynesians, at least two thousand have been introduced since the time of Captain Cook. Some have been accidental, but most have been intentional for use as ornament (especially orchids) or food or for forestation. Insects represent another huge category of new species numbering more than thirty-three hundred, the vast majority arriving after 1779. In addition to those mentioned earlier, like mosquitoes, cockroaches, and ants, there would now be an army of armyworms, scorpions, centipedes, spiders, bees and bumblebees, forty more species of ants, and many, many more. Regarding extinctions, the best (worst) examples are birds and tree snails. Of all the birds that have suffered extinction in Hawai'i, about two-thirds went extinct after 1779. Some 75 percent of Hawai'i's tree snails are also gone, 10 percent before Western contact, 65 percent after.

Particularly destructive introductions after 1779 include a number of smothering plants such as *Miconia* species, banana poka, and strawberry guava; the giant African snail; coquí frogs of chirping fame; cane toads that are poisonous; two more rats from Europe; a mongoose to control the rats; and hosts of feral ungulates including goats, sheep, deer, and cattle, all causing immense erosion to upland habitats. Hawai'i's freshwater streams and lakes haven't escaped the onslaught of introductions either. More than fifty new species now exist in Hawaiian freshwater habitats compared to only five fish, two shrimps, and several mollusks that are endemic.

Interestingly, the marine environment in Hawai'i has endured few impacts caused by human contact, virtually all after 1779. Eight species of fish have been introduced, but only three are very successful (*ta'ape*, *toau*, and *roi*). The worst introductions have been five kinds of exotic algae (*Hypnea*, *Kapaphycus*, *Gracilaria*, *Acanthophora*, and mudweed), but all of these are limited primarily to shallow-water habitats either on reef flats or within bays, most famously Kāne'ohe Bay. Of all the invertebrates that have arrived in Hawai'i on ship bottoms, only one, the soft coral *Carijoa riisei* has reached pest abundance levels but only in dimly lit environments (pier pilings, wharfs, and deep reefs swept by strong current).

SUSTAINABILITY OR PARADISE LOST?

Given the needs of the human beings to survive and prosper in Hawai'i and their lack of awareness particularly in the early years after Western contact, what kind of future can we look forward to in the new century? History has proved that the Hawaiians were relatively good stewards of the land for many centuries, but theirs was a subsistence economy. Today our population is four or seven times larger than it was during the height of the Hawaiian Kingdom. Our economy has become global and interdependent. Prosperity must now be added to subsistence. Taken together, it is clear they will define new limits to island growth. Will the future bring the best of times, or will our standard of living slowly begin to fall? The answer may depend on the ability of society to identify and accept limits to growth.

Two stories that might be compared could help answer the question. The first one is about the exploitation that took place on Laysan Island in the early twentieth century. The second is a story that I will call "What We Must Do to Sustain the Future."

The first story is about Max Schlemmer, who is notorious in Hawaiian history for almost destroying the entire ecosystem on Laysan Island in the Northwestern Hawaiian Islands. Max Schlemmer was born in Germany in 1856. In 1871 he immigrated to the United States and from there to Hawai'i in 1885. In 1894 he was hired to oversee a guano-mining operation on Laysan Island. He arrived there with his sixteen-year-old wife and three children, and during his tenure of almost twenty years there, he fathered five more.

Laysan Island is an almost flat coral island. Earlier in its history it was an atoll, but its former lagoon has been filled in by massive deposits of wave-washed sand and coral rubble, creating a hypersaline lake. For this reason, Laysan Island is a seabird paradise. Before Max Schlemmer got there, it was home to more than ten million seabirds, including the largest reported colony of black-footed albatross in the world, as well as seventeen other seabird species. For about five million years, Laysan's bird populations have been excreting guano, thereby building rich deposits of phosphate fertilizer, the source of the commercial mining operation. In 1896 Max Schlemmer was promoted to mining superintendent, and soon after he was able to procure a fifteen-year lease from the Hawaiian Land Use Commission in Honolulu to exploit Laysan's resources. Armed with entrepreneurial greed and almost complete ecological ignorance, Max Schlemmer set about to take dominion over "his" kingdom.

During the next fifteen years, his team of workers wiped out the guano deposits, shipping about 500 tons per year to Honolulu. But guano was not his only quarry. The Schlemmer team would slaughter tens of thousands of albatross birds every year and ship their feathers to Japan for the millinery trade (figure 61). Not only that, he sold literally tons of albatross eggs (figure 62) for the manufacture of photographic emulsions to various world markets. If all of this wasn't enough, Max Schlemmer introduced rabbits to Laysan Island in 1902 with the alleged aim of creating a meat canning factory. He envisioned Laysan as a rabbit ranch. At another point, he tried to start a coconut plantation, but that venture, like all the others, failed. Over the years, the rabbits multiplied and eventually wiped out about twenty-five species of plants and drove three endemic birds to extinction (a millerbird, a rail, and a honeycreeper). Basically all Schlemmer's operations and schemes came to an end when President Theodore Roosevelt set aside the NWHI under the legal protection of a bird reservation. Schlemmer continued operations for a time but was soon arrested for poaching and was tried in a Honolulu court. For some reason, he was acquitted.

In 1923, a scientific expedition (the Tanager Expedition) visited Laysan Island. What they found there was a sandy wasteland. The ecosystem had been

ABOVE
FIGURE 61.
Before the arrival of Max Schlemmer on Laysan Island, albatross birds were extremely abundant.

LEFT
FIGURE 62.
Albatross egg–collecting operations on Laysan Island in the early 1900s.

virtually destroyed. Several hundred rabbits were still alive, but they eventually starved to death. And so ends our story of Max Schlemmer at Laysan Island. Fortunately it is a story of the times, but hopefully it is one that will not be repeated.

Max Schlemmer's rise and fall on Laysan Island might be a microcosmic example of how complete replacement of Hawaiian traditions by Western values could affect the future of the Hawaiian Islands. His story therefore contains some important lessons. Foremost, it is clear that island ecosystems are extremely fragile, and their resources are not inexhaustible. In chapter 5, we learned that these vulnerabilities are the result of isolation and small size. The Hawaiians may have intuitively sensed that their peak population numbers had exceeded the carrying capacity of the islands. In any case, their behavior during peak population years resulted in stricter *kapu*, possibly infanticide, human sacrifice, and warfare. All are possible reasons why their numbers may have contracted even before Western contact. So how then will the second story play out? What must we do now to sustain the future of Hawai'i?

As mentioned above, the population in Hawai'i today is 1.4 million people about four or seven times larger than peak numbers in the Hawaiian Kingdom. But it is also clear that the rules of a subsistence economy and its carrying capacity no longer apply. Nevertheless, our ecosystems are just as fragile today, and many of our resources are just as exhaustible as they ever were. To date, population growth in Hawai'i is steadily increasing, and ultimately it may become our biggest problem.

On the other hand, since the days of Max Schlemmer, the pendulum of change is definitely swinging in the opposite direction. Many steps are being taken to protect or conserve Hawai'i's environment. In 2001, President William Clinton created by Executive Order a NWHI Coral Reef Ecosystem Reserve that afforded abundant protection of its resources in the three- to fifty-mile offshore zone. In 2006, near the end of his second term, President George W. Bush reclassified the NWHI a national monument, Papahānaumokuākea. In the main Hawaiian Islands, the federal government has created a whale sanctuary that protects Hawai'i's humpback whales. The Western Pacific Regional Fishery Management Council has developed an Archipelagic Fishery Ecosystem Plan and management plans for Hawai'i's five major fisheries (pelagics, bottom fish, lobsters, coral reef ecosystems, and precious corals). The state of Hawai'i has also created ten Marine Life Conservation Districts (MLCDs) in which fishing is prohibited or restricted. These are but a few of the positive steps that have been taken to protect Hawai'i's environment, and yet a lot more needs to be done.

Considering lessons of the past and what might be done to insure Hawai'i's future, at least three major actions would seem obvious although not simple.

First, stop the introductions except for species of clear environmental benefit that pose no negative threat. Second, stop the extinctions, easier said than done. Third, strengthen existing management structures in the state and at the federal level. Within this category of action there are dozens of steps that can or should be taken. I will list a few:

1. Create more Marine Life Conservation Districts. At the present time, less than 1 percent of the coastline in the Main Hawaiian Islands is protected from overfishing.

2. Stop overfishing and enforce existing fish and game regulations and institute a recreational fishing license. Over the last century, Hawai'i's nearshore fisheries in the MHI have declined by 70 to 90 percent.

3. Stop destructive fishing practices such as gill netting, the use of clorox, and scuba spear fishing at night.

4. Encourage more aquaculture and open-ocean fish farming.

5. Reinstate some of the traditional methods of conservation practiced by the Hawaiians, such as fishponds and a *kapu* system.

6. On the land, the state Department of Land and Natural Resources (DLNR) should change many of its policies. One of the most damaging has to do with invasive hoofed animals (pigs, goats, sheep, deer, and cattle). The existing state policy is to shoot for population control with the help of the hunters. But in reality, the policy is to "release and forget" the animals. It is a policy driven by lack of staffing, lack of funding, and lots of politics.

7. The Division of Aquatic Resources and the marine sections of the Division of Conservation and Resource Enforcement should be split off from DLNR and placed into a new department; the Department of the Oceans.

8. For the land, industries such as agriculture, the military, and tourism should be favored because they do not directly lead to permanent increases in population and because their presence prevents large tracts of land from being developed for housing and other commercial development.

9. Finally, population growth overall needs to be controlled to the extent possible within existing laws and individual rights. Perhaps the best approach to address this problem is through zoning practices.

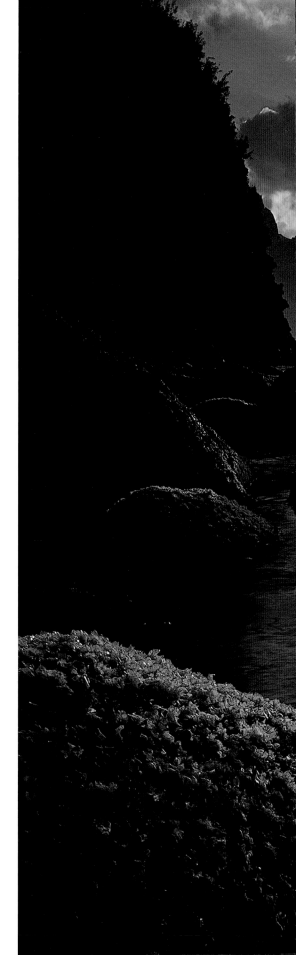

In summary, the above list is far from complete of what must be done to sustain Hawai'i's future, but it also suggests the philosophic direction in which our pendulum should swing. Hawai'i stands at a sustainability crossroad. Will its natural beauty succumb to overpopulation and overdevelopment, or will a new wave of environmental awareness overcome the forces of unrestrained growth? It is time to actually confront the difficult actions that need to be taken to sustain Hawai'i's ecological complexity and natural grandeur. Hawai'i's future will be decided by choices, choices made by its people and by the vision exercised by its leaders. Will the Hawaiian Islands remain a tropical paradise, or will their future be a story of a paradise lost? In the beginning, Madam Pele blessed her islands, but in the future, her blessings should not be forgotten. It is a Hawaiian vision of a new dawn.

FIGURE 63. Since the beginning, about seventy million years ago, the Hawaiian hot spot has given birth to 107 volcanoes. Their future depends on human choice, to either preserve paradise or allow continuous unrestrained economic growth. It is a choice between sustainability or paradise lost.

ACKNOWLEDGMENTS

I would first like to thank Island Heritage for the opportunity to pull together almost fifty years of my research work on shallow- and deep-water corals and the origin and history of the Hawaiian Archipelago. Numerous colleagues and students are too many to thank individually, although I do wish to single out several people who have played major roles in the story. With respect to my graduate studies in ecology and oceanography, my major professor at Scripps Institution of Oceanography, Dr. E. William Fager, basically taught me how to think; always take a long world view; but then focus the thought, simplify, integrate, and synthesize. Much earlier on, my mother encouraged me to follow my instincts and natural curiosity. In my undergraduate studies, my zoology professor, Max Silvernale, inspired me to understand the fascinating evolutionary relationships between humans and all other forms of life. After graduate school, I began a long career at the University of Hawai'i at a time when plate tectonics and the Hawaiian hot spot had just been discovered. I thank Dr. John Craven, dean of Marine Programs at the University of Hawai'i, and Jack Davidson, director of the University of Hawai'i Sea Grant College Program, for the financial support that funded years of research on the origin of the Hawaiian Islands and the evolution of its coral reefs.

In the course of this work, I borrowed or tested concepts and theories of Charles Darwin, Harry Hess, Robert Dietz, and John Tuzo Wilson to formulate the Darwin Point hypothesis. I thank Steve Dollar, Bill Whorster, Randy Sneider, Nancy Jones, and the pilots of the University of Hawai'i submersibles, Boh

Bartko and Terry Kerby, for helping to collect and analyze the Darwin Point data. I would also mention my experience of surfing in Hawai'i, since waves are extremely important in controlling the ecology of shallow-water reef-building corals. My personal experience of surfing and diving (snorkeling, scuba, and submersible observations) has exposed my "mind's eye" to the intermixture of natural forces that shape marine ecosystems. On land, Harold Starns taught me to apply the same method of personal observation to understand the geological history of Hawai'i. Alexander Agassiz said it best in about 1872, "Study nature, not books." In brief, I am indebted to many, many naturalists for their research on which I have relied to write this book. To name a few: Drs. Sidney Townsley, Alison Kay, Lu Eldredge, William Easton, Tony Jones, Chip Fletcher, Alan Ziegler, Chuck Blay, John Culliney, James Maragos, and Richard Fairbanks. Other scholars or students of the sea that I have relied upon include Patrick Kirch, Ben Finney, and Nainoa Thompson.

Finally, I wish to thank all the staff at Island Heritage for their editorial assistance in the production of this book. My wish is that other oceanographers, biologists, and geologists will follow and fill in the blanks or rewrite sections of the book based on new and more accurate information. In the end, we can all be thankful to the maker of the Hawaiian Islands, be it the gods Prometheus, or Madam Pele, or Kanaloa, or simply the natural laws of the universe, and perhaps also to that unknown force known as First Cause. However created, Hawai'i is truly a paradise on Earth.

GLOSSARY

'a'ā lava. Hawaiian lava flows that have a rough, clinker, or rubbly surface

adaptive radiation. The evolution of new biological species due to natural selection and environmental adaptation

ahupua'a. A watershed or pie-shaped wedge of land in Hawai'i that generally descends from the mountaintop to the shoreline

alien species. A non-native organism, sometimes called a nonindigenous, exotic, or introduced species

archipelago. A chain of islands in an ocean or sea

atoll. A circular coral island and reef that nearly or entirely encloses a lagoon

Austronesian. A family of Malayo-Polynesian languages spoken three thousand to four thousand years ago in remote Oceania

continental drift. The gradual movement of continents due to plate tectonics and seafloor spreading

convection cells. Huge plumes of lava that circulate within the Earth that help drive sea-floor spreading

core. The molten center of the Earth

Darwin Point. A threshold geographic place or depth where coral reefs or coral islands drown because coral growth cannot keep up with sea level rise or island subsidence

diaspora. The great dispersal of Polynesian people throughout Oceania by way of voyaging canoes

disharmonic. A term used to describe a biological community that is undersaturated or only partially filled with species

diversity. Variety, or the measure of the different kinds of species in a biological community

endemic. Species native to a particular environment that occur nowhere else in the world

exotic. Introduced species

fauna. Organisms that belong to the animal kingdom

flora. Organisms that belong to the plant kingdom

founder effect. Effects associated with the first species to colonize a new environment such as islands

generalized. A species that is adapted to broad differences in the environment, widespread, hardy

Gondwana. A hypothetical continent that existed on earth about 180 million years ago that split up to form South America, Africa, India, and Australia

Great *Mahele*. The great division of land in Hawai'i in the 1840s that reapportioned land among crown, government, chiefs, and commoners

guyot. A drowned atoll or flat-topped seamount

hot spot. A melting anomaly in the crust of the Earth where volcanic islands are produced

indigenous. Native species that occur widely throughout a region

Indo-West Pacific (IWP). Islands and archipelagos in Southeast Asia

invertebrate. Animals without backbones, soft-bodied

islet. A small island

isostacy. A condition of equal buoyancy or balance between different segments of the Earth's crust

isotopic dating. A method of dating rocks or fossils based on known rates of decay of their radioactive atoms

kapu. A system of cultural taboos in Hawai'i; prohibition

konohiki. Hawaiian native rights that pertain to special uses of certain resources or lands

K-T impact. A cosmic impact on Earth caused by collision from an asteroid or comet that hit southern Mexico about sixty-five million years ago, causing widespread biotic extinctions

Lapita culture. An early (around four thousand years ago) Polynesian culture noted for its distinctive pottery first discovered in Lapita, New Caledonia

Laurasia. A hypothetical continent that existed on earth about 180 million years ago that split up to form North America and Eurasia

lineage. A line of descent that traces the genetic origin of an organism

lithosphere. The crust of the Earth, divided into about twenty large crustal plates

mantle. The layer of the Earth between the core and the crust (lithosphere)

mass wasting. Erosional processes that diminish the mass of an existing island or seamount

Miocene. A geological time zone that lasted between five and twenty-four million years ago

natural selection. A process of biological evolution that leads to the survival of the "most fit" species

nautical mile. A nautical mile is 1.15 times longer than a statute mile

niche. The "place" an organism occupies in nature that defines where it is found and how it functions in a community

***pāhoehoe* lava.** Hawaiian lava flows that have a smooth, ropy, curved, or billowy surface

paleomagnetism. The magnetic field in a volcanic rock that is fixed when it solidifies

Pangaea. A hypothetical universal continent in which all modern continents on Earth were once joined

Papahānaumokuākea. A 140,000 square mile Marine National Monument encompassing the Northwestern Hawaiian Islands from Nihoa to Kure Atoll

posterosional eruption. Small volcanic eruptions that occur long after an original volcano has undergone extensive erosion

primogeniture. A Polynesian cultural practice of inheritance that favors the firstborn

propagule. Any structure such as a bud or egg that aids in the dispersal of a species

rift zone. An area on the Earth's surface that is splitting apart or fissuring

seamount. An undersea mountain

specialized. A species that is narrowly adapted to its environment

speciation. The formation of a new species through natural selection

species. A population of organisms capable of interbreeding and producing fertile offspring

subduction. The submergence of a portion of the Earth's crust into a trench or below a continent caused by seafloor spreading and convergence of crustal (plate) boundaries

Tethys Sea. A primordial sea that separated the ancient land masses of Gondwana and Laurasia

tragedy of the commons. The social tragedy that ensues from increasing competition for a limited or decreasing resource

REFERENCES AND FURTHER READING

Culliney, John L. *Islands in a Far Sea: The Fate of Nature in Hawai'i*. Honolulu: University of Hawai'i Press, 2006.

Evenhuis, Neal L., and Lucius G. Eldredge. *Natural History of Nihoa and Necker Islands*. Honolulu: Bishop Museum Press, 2004.

Grigg, Richard W. "Darwin Point: A Threshold for Atoll Formation." *Coral Reefs* 1, no 1 (1982): 29–34.

———. "Paleoceanography of Coral Reefs in the Hawaiian-Emperor Chain." *Science* 240, no. 4860 (24 Jun 1988): 1,737–1,743.

Grigg, Richard W., Jeffery Polovina, Alan. M. Friedlander, and Steven O. Rohmann. "Biology of Coral Reefs in the Northwestern Hawaiian Islands." *Coral Reefs of the USA* 1 (2008): 573–594.

Herter, Eric, ed. *Discovery: The Hawaiian Odyssey*. Honolulu: Bishop Museum Press, 1993.

Hoover, John P. *Hawai'i's Sea Creatures: A Guide to Hawai'i's Marine Invertebrates*. Honolulu: Mutual Publishing, 1998.

Jackson, E.D., I. Koizumi, et al. *Initial Reports of the Deep Sea Drilling Project, Leg* 55. Washington, DC: U.S. Government Printing Office, 1980.

Kay, E. Alison, ed. *A Natural History of the Hawaiian Islands: Selected Readings II*. Honolulu: University of Hawai'i Press, 1994.

Kirch, Patrick V. "Polynesian Prehistory: Cultural Adaptation in Island Ecosystems," *American Scientist*, January–February 1980, 39–48.

Kirch, Patrick V., and Jean-Louis Rallu, eds. *The Growth and Collapse of Pacific Island Societies: Archeological and Demographic Perspectives*. Honolulu: University of Hawai'i Press, 2008.

MacDonald, Gordon A., and Agatin T. Abbott. *Volcanoes in the Sea: The Geology of Hawai'i*. Honolulu: University of Hawai'i Press, 1970.

Morgan, W. Jason. "Deep Mantle Convection Plumes and Plate Motions." *AAPG Bulletin* 56, no. 2 (February 1972): 203–213.

Oliver, Douglas. *Polynesia in Early Historic Times*. Honolulu: The Bess Press Inc., 2002.

Rauzon, Mark J. *Isles of Refuge: Wildlife and History of the Northwestern Hawaiian Islands*. Honolulu: University of Hawai'i Press, 2001.

Staples, George W., and Robert H. Cowie, eds. *Hawai'i's Invasive Species: A Guide to the Invasive Plants and Animals in the Hawaiian Islands*. Honolulu: Mutual Publishing, 2001.

Yamamoto, Mike N., and Annette W. Tagawa. *Hawai'i's Native and Exotic Freshwater Animals*. Honolulu: Mutual Publishing, 2000.

Ziegler, Alan C. *Hawaiian Natural History, Ecology, and Evolution*. Honolulu: University of Hawai'i Press, 2002.

FIGURE CREDITS

CHAPTER 4

Figure 24. page 36: Brooks G. Bays, Jr.
Figure 25. page 39: Adapted from R.W. Grigg artwork.
Figure 26. page 42: R.W. Grigg
Figure 27. page 43: R.W. Grigg
Figure 28. page 45: R.W. Grigg
Figure 29. page 46: R.W. Grigg
Figure 30. page 47: Adapted from G. Rotondo, MS Thesis, University of Hawai'i, 1980.
Figure 31. page 49: R.W. Grigg
Figure 32. page 49: R.W. Grigg
Figure 33. page 49: National Oceanic and Atmospheric Administration (NOAA)

CHAPTER 5

Figure 34. page 52: Island Heritage Archive
Figure 35. page 54: Don Davis, NASA
Figure 36. page 56: R.W. Grigg
Figure 37. page 58: R.W. Grigg
Figure 38. page 59: George Balaz
Figure 39. page 60: Kevin A. Edwards
Figure 40. page 61: Ron Dahlquist
Figure 41. page 62: H. Douglas Pratt
Figure 42. page 65: Adapted from H.W. Menard and E.L. Hamilton, *Paleogeography of the Tropical Pacific*.
Figure 43. page 66: Brooks G. Bays, Jr.
Figure 44. page 67: Adapted from D.R. Stoddart, Biogeography of the Tropical Pacific, *Pacific Science*, 46, 1992.
Figure 45. page 69: idreamphoto/Shutterstock.com
Figure 46. page 69: R.W. Grigg
Figure 47. page 69: R.W. Grigg
Figure 48. page 69: R.W. Grigg
Figure 49. page 70: R.W. Grigg
Figure 50. page 70: R.W. Grigg
Figure 51. page 71: Adapted from R.W. Grigg et al., *Coral Reefs of the USA*, Springer, 2008.
Figure 52. page 72: R.W. Grigg
Figure 53. page 76-77: Graham Osborne

CHAPTER 6

Figure 54. page 78: Island Heritage Archive, original artwork by Don Robinson.
Figure 55. page 81: Island Heritage Archive
Figure 56. page 82: Adapted from Patrick Kirch, *Scientific American*, 1980.
Figure 57. page 85: Adapted from Patrick Kirch, *Scientific American*, 1980.
Figure 58. page 86: Adapted from Patrick Kirch, *The Growth and Collapse of Pacific Island Societies*, University of Hawai'i Press, 2007.
Figure 59. page 87: Hawai'i State Archives
Figure 60. page 90: Based on Hawai'i State Census and estimates by Captains James Cook and George Dixon.
Figure 61. page 93: Hawai'i State Archives
Figure 62. page 93: Hawai'i State Archives
Figure 63. page 96-97: Graham Osborne

INDEX

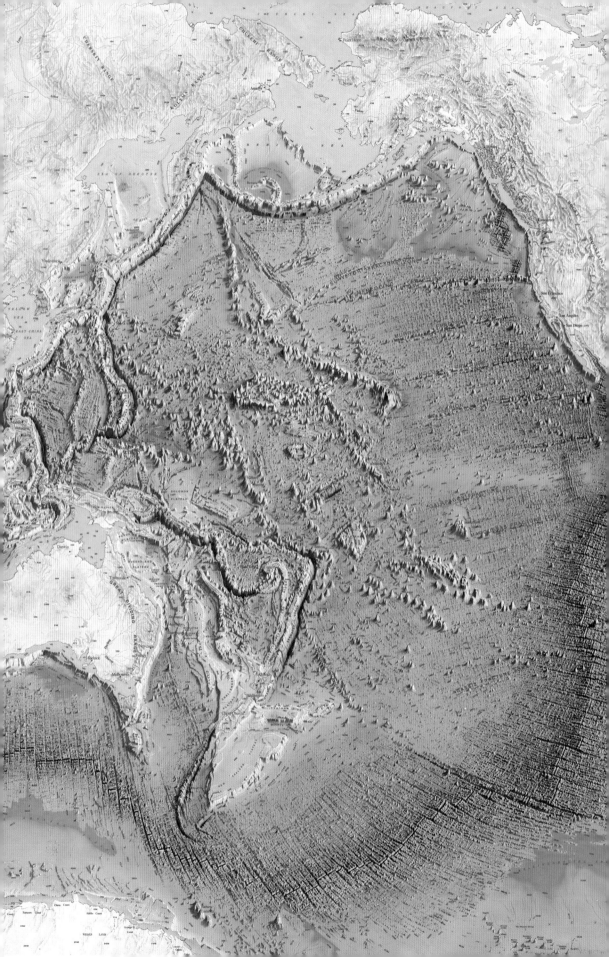